KU-531-528

# The QE2 Cook Book

· GRETEL BEER ·

Photographs by Laurie Evans

ANDRE
DEUTSCH

685039

MURAY COUNCIL

Department of Technical

& Leisure Services

641.5

First published in 1999 by
André Deutsch Ltd
76 Dean Street
London W1V 5HA

www.vci.co.uk

Text copyright © Gretel Beer 1999

The right of Gretel Beer to be identified as the author of this work
has been asserted by her in accordance with the Copyright, Designs and Patents Act 1988

All rights reserved. This book is sold subject to the condition that it may not be reproduced,
stored in a retrieval system or transmitted in any form or by any means, electronic, mechanical, photocopying,
recording or otherwise without the Publisher's prior consent

A catalogue for this book is available from the British Library

ISBN 0 233 99490 4

Typeset by Derek Doyle & Associates
Mold, Flintshire
Printed and bound in the UK by Butler and Tanner, Frome and London

1 3 5 7 9 10 8 6 4 2

Design by Rob Kelland
Photography by Laurie Evans
Edited by Winifred Carr

The Publisher would like to thank
Le Creuset and Villeroy & Boch for the supply of equipment.

# CONTENTS

# Introduction

## By Charles Hennessy

When, as a young man, I first traversed that mother of all sea-routes, the North Atlantic, it was in the care of those almost equally legendary seafarers, Cunard. I was travelling First Class what's more, and on the mighty *Queen Mary* no less, and, to make the pleasure complete, I wasn't paying. That was the burden, or privilege, of the grand London advertizing agency for which I worked – if that is the word for what we so-called 'creatives' did – and it was jolly nice of them, considering that I had shortly before handed in my notice.

The mecca of advertizing in those far off mid-1950s was New York, and having decided to worship at the source, I had dramatically resigned, conveying, as I hoped, the clear impression that I would bravely make my own way there, whatever the hardships. The result, not entirely unexpected, was that the Chairman of the Board, who until then had hardly addressed a word to me, invited me to lunch at his club, the Garrick (good house claret, *en carafe*). His proposal was that I should spend a year on Madison Avenue, acquiring wisdom at the fount, and then return to spread the good word. 'You can fly or go by boat,' he said, genially. Flying, in those days, was by bumpy turbo-prop, *through* the weather, with a stopover in some shed in Gander, wherever that was. 'How do *you* go?' I asked innocently. The grizzled Chairman raised a wiry eyebrow over his pince-nez. 'What kind of a fool do you take me for?' he asked, although, being a sailing man, the noun he employed was somewhat saltier.

Thus it was that I found myself acquiring a steamer trunk, a kind of heavy metal combined wardrobe and chest of drawers that was *de rigueur* for the serious traveller, and slapping and tying on it those covetable labels, in smart Cunard red and black on white, that bore the thrilling legend, 'QUEEN MARY', followed by the lofty admonition, 'FIRST CLASS'. The special Boat Train from Victoria was First Class too: lower-ranked passengers had already been embarked and, though comfortably-enough, I fondly supposed, stashed away out of sight.

Arrival on board at Southampton instantly evoked the question famously posed by the Canadian-born comedienne Bea Lillie (who travelled in her other persona as the English Lady Peel): 'What time does this place get to New York?' My stateroom – none of your pokey cabins here – was (on the Chairman's advice) on 'A' Deck, and next to that of the Duke and Duchess of Windsor. To be more accurate, it was next to the stateroom of the Windsors' servants, which was next to their employers. To be absolutely truthful, it was next to the Windsors' *dogs'* stateroom, which was … but that was good enough for me.

Dinner that night – with the Duchess looking chalkily too thin and too rich in the first of a parade of Balenciagas – was in the kind of pillared ballroom found in the grander hotels, which were then the social centres of the world-class cities (my agency's directors routinely lunched down the road at the Savoy, and *signed* the bill). The food – apart from the permanent centrepiece of a vast bowl of ice with a family-size pot of glittering black caviar at its heart and a large spoon helpfully dunked in it – was of the kind served in such places, anywhere in the world, whatever the

5

climate or the local cuisine. There was smoked (Irish) salmon, turtle soup with sherry, gelée mandrilène, gnocchis (whatever happened to gnocchis?), baked York ham, lots of roasts and game, soufflé Rothschild, bombe Jubilée and, after the dessert, now-vanished savouries like Welsh Rarebit (pronounced 'rabbit'). It was the kind of cuisine ('Oh no, not caviar *again*', said Mrs James Wrigley II of Chicago on the third night out) with which this pre-tourism kind of traveller – aristocrat, banker, diplomat, publisher, cardsharp – was comfortable, the kind they could count on finding at the Adler, the Waldorf Astoria, Shepheards, Raffles and the various Ritzses at which they arrived by Wagons Lits or chauffeured Hispano Suiza. It was all right with me too. But it was not the kind of cuisine of which you could make a cook book, and if you could, I wouldn't have been a buyer, even then, in my state of (relative) culinary innocence.

The conspicuous consumption – lunch was on the same scale as dinner – went on for five days and nights, with a steaming mug of Bovril (which, as we had informed the world from our advertizing agency, 'prevents that sinking feeling') brought to your deckchair by a white-jacketed Cunard steward at mid-morning, and afternoon tea to rival that of the Palm Court at the Ritz, and post-prandial port and brandy in the ballroom. An unplanned bonus was New Year's Eve. Since the clocks were put back an hour each midnight, having seen the thing in with streamers, champagne, Auld Lang Syne and kisses, we immediately started all over again.

All of this wining and dining, the bracing promenades, the deck quoits, the nightly hectic bingo, the dinner-jacketing in best midnight blue and the parading of tonight's new ballgown, the dancing, was the privilege of those who had paid the First Class fare. There may have been high-jinks going on below deck, on a numerically vaster scale, but we knew nothing of it, and passengers in other classes, as they explored the great ship,

found themselves confronted by doors marked 'First Class passengers only beyond this point'. (My Chairman had thoughtfully informed me that the girls in First would be heavily chaperoned, but that the bars on the lower deck were open to privileged chaps like me and that, since passengers in other classes could visit First only on invitation, a reconnaissance, wearing the give-away black tie, could be fruitful: his plan was sound but, sadly, as I was about to make my bid I became sea-sick).

What this five-day, non-stop entertainment needed was a grand finale, and on the last morning, at dawn, it got one – big-time. Someone once said that, on a plane, you go to places, on a ship, the places come to you. Up on Promenade Deck, above us the red and black funnel blasting a welcome, we stood silently as the great liner nosed down the Hudson and the Statue of Liberty (that national symbol that seems to belong to everyone, whatever his nation) loomed towards us, arm upraised, and the towers of Manhattan, that giant cut-out so familiar from movies, loomed ever larger through the mist: earth's greatest stage set, the sight of a lifetime, and, like the food, included in the price of the ticket.

All of this, of course, is water under the great ship's bridge. I have driven past a moored hulk that claims to be the great liner, sadly Long Beached in California, but it didn't fool me. That life, those days are gone forever. History. Or so I thought. Then, not long ago, I had the chance to board another Cunarder of great reputation, and in Cunard's home port of Southampton too. (The First Class Boat Train has gone with the windjammer – but you can take the fabled Orient Express instead). The moment I stepped off the gangway on to the scrubbed deck of the QE2, it all – or most of it – came back. It felt, to use Miss Lillie's word, like a place, all right, but if it too, evokes the grand hotel, it is one in which you feel immediately at home – even though in more luxurious surroundings than at home. Would

QE2

everything else – the many pleasurable and permissible self-indulgences of a sea voyage – measure up to my memories?

Here is what the Irish journalist, Philip Nolan, had to say, reassuringly, about that: 'You don't cruise the Atlantic on this ship – you literally eat your way across the ocean, marking progress not by latitude or longitude but by another course finished, another bottle drained ...' Ah! And what's this? 'Captain's parties'; 'Champagne nights in the Wardroom'; 'three of the five nights are classed as formal'*. And then? 'Passing Coney Island and under the Verragano Narrows Bridge, up the Hudson and into Manhattan'.

The *QE2* has assumed the mantle of legend discarded by the older Queen. The *Mary* sailed the Atlantic for thirty-one years, making 1,001 crossings. By June 1995, the *QE2* had completed its 1,000th voyage. 'There's nothing of the old lady about the new *Queen Elizabeth 2*', reported the *Daily Telegraph* on its launch. 'She is smart, crisp and modern, using new colours and fabrics and materials'. *The Times* recorded that 'the impression is of good 1960s hotel design compared with the good 1930s design of the old Queens. Moulded wood, wrought metal, folkweave and damask are out, plastic, tweed, leather are in.' (That was then: there has been much refurbishment since and an elaborate pre-millennium refit in November 1999 promises, among other embellishments, acres of Axminster and clusters of crystal chandeliers.)

All this is fine, but, as the ship set sail and I heard again in my (ah, yes) *stateroom* the familiar, friendly creak and groan of teak, it seemed to me that it was Gary Buchanan, author of a fine history of the ship**, who has put his finger on the Full Steam Ahead button. The *QE2*, he writes, is 'a conduit to rekindling memories of a lost era.' The

ship, says Buchanan, evokes a period when time was not so precious, when crossing the Atlantic was measured in days, not hours, when the journey, not the destination, was the important thing. Indeed, the *QE2 is* the destination, a resort in its own right, self-contained and self-sufficient. This plenitude, of course, is all the more important now that the great liner regularly transforms itself into a cruise ship, with voyages that can last up to a hundred days (during which, Cunard confidently claim, no dish is ever repeated).

If the *QE2* is a place, it is a small, spruce, immaculately-appointed town – you'll find it in the RAC Guide – and within those thirteen decks are all the amenities you would expect to find: library (the biggest afloat), crèche, doctor's surgery, dentist, hospital, cinema, theatre, hairdresser and beauty salon, boutiques, travel agent, dancing class, gym, bars (seven of them), photographic studio, printing press, kennels, and pools – and a health spa.

And it's Open City. As the journalist Jonathan Brown joyously declared, 'Democracy is alive and well and living it up on the *QE2*. The boundaries which exist in normal society evaporate the moment you step aboard.' Everybody is available to everybody else. You can wander where you want, when you want. The pecking order, in-so-far as it exists, is literally that: you are where you eat. There are five fine restaurants in town – as well as a rather superior self-service brasserie – and the one to which you are assigned is decided by the price you chose to pay for your ticket.

Clearly, Cunard had evolved – but then so had I. From the wide-eyed not-so-innocent young man-on-the-make who boarded the *Queen Mary* all those aeons ago, I had become a more worldly-wise fellow who had lived in Paris for 17 years,

---

*Transatlantic crossings now include six nights, of which three are formal.

**Queen Elizabeth 2 – Sailing into the Millennium.* Published by Maritime Heritage.

QE2

explored the restaurants, great and small, of France and parlayed the knowledge there acquired into a second career as food writer and restaurant reviewer (somebody has to do it) with *The Times* and *Bon Appétit*. The Captain, it was clear, was a splendid man and ran a fine ship, but it was the Hotel Manager who was responsible for keeping the passengers happy, and I found John Duffy's philosophy immediately engaging: 'The way to the passengers' hearts is through their tummies. We offer them the tastiest dishes it is possible to prepare. And if they want something that isn't on the menu, then our chefs will cook it for them. And that's a promise.' It is one that is kept – I put him to the test.

Those coddled passengers heroically chomp and glug their way through 3,200 eggs, 60 lbs of smoked salmon and 200 bottles of champagne *every day*. Yes, but what about that very symbol of luxury and gracious living, those salty black diamonds from the Caspian, so abundantly available on the great Cunarders of yore (in First Class, that is)? Not to worry. The *QE2* corners more of the sublime stuff than any other establishment on land, sea or in the air. Passengers get through 2,409 lbs of caviar a year – and would probably manage more if the precious cargo wasn't kept locked in a metal cage in a storeroom, entry to which requires four signatures.

For me, the Cunard evolution – apart from the welcome democratization – was most visible in the cuisine. As in other fields of commerce, throughout the Western world, restaurants had adapted to the effects of globalization. Freed from the chains of national tradition, faced with customers who were more travelled, better educated in culinary matters (and who watched their diets), chefs had begun to lighten, simplify and, literally, spice up their cuisines. Touches of Thai, Indian, Japanese and California were gratefully added to the classic dishes and welcomed by the newly-enlightened clientele –

and by such august arbiters as the inspectors of the Michelin Guide.

If the cuisine on the *Queen Mary* sought to emulate – in richness, familiarity and quantity – that of the great hotel restaurants, that of the *QE2* has quite different goals. 'Expectations are high: customers measure our restaurants against the Michelin-starred restaurants they frequent on shore,' said Karl Winkler, the ship's Executive Chef. He is himself the very model of modern eclecticism: born (like the compiler of this mouthwatering book) in Austria, he has cooked in New York, Korea and London (the Ritz), is married to an Englishwoman and has been travelling with Cunard since 1973. He supervizes the five chefs de cuisine, who are rotated to ensure that the quality of the cooking in the ritzy Queen's Grill is the same as that in the jollier Lido. When he joined, he was the only non-British member of the kitchen staff: today, reflecting the ethnic influence on the menus, they are a diverse mix of fifteen to twenty different nationalities.

The leading guidebooks concur on the result of their work. The QE2 is the only ship to be awarded five stars by the RAC, and, from that house of many languages, the *Berlitz Guide to Cruising* for 1998 not only concluded that this was 'without doubt the finest experience of dining at sea' but exclaimed, 'Well done, Cunard, for bringing the culinary art to the highest maritime level!' (Berlitz thought it advisable, however, to remind its readers that the QE2 was 'the last of the great ocean liners and the only way to cross the North Atlantic with pace and grace'). As for the famous red guide referred to by Mr Winkler, the *Daily Telegraph* recently concluded that, of the five restaurants on board, 'the best is equivalent to Michelin two–three star.' Praise indeed.

For all the solid merits of the grand hotel cuisine of the ancient *Queen*, you would never have found on its menu anything with the eclectic appeal of Chilled Fennel Essence with Pernod, or Chilled Cranberry Soup with Aquavit, to be followed, say, by Salmon Tartare with Yoghurt and Dill Sauce, hotly pursued by a Seared Sea Bass with Nicoise Relish and Bouillabaisse Sauce. And then perhaps a nibble of Thyme Gnocchi (so *that's* what happened to gnocchi) and Apple Mint Chutney? Roast Quail filled with Foie Gras on a bed of Green Lentils with Shallot Confit, anyone? You can tell this ship has been around. Shiver me Timberlands, the old *Queen Mary* was never like this! Thanks, I'm ready now for my soup: Red Berry Soup, that is, infused with Red Wine, topped with Raspberry Sorbet (from the great three-star Lameloise, in Chagny).

One journalist, Alan Air, was reluctant to take the air: 'One QE2 [TV] channel is devoted to the view from the bridge. I couldn't be bothered going on deck to see the ship leave port. I would watch it on the box, sip champagne and pore over the menus, the hardest choice you ever have to make on board. If only all life was thus …'

Always worth going on deck for though, as I had all those years ago, is the arrival in New York. You can still experience the rare thrill of ghosting up the mighty Hudson at dawn, the funnel in Cunard red and black livery above you blasting its salute, the world's best-known city scape before you as you nose into the sleeping heart of Manhattan. As Jonathan Brown put it, 'Everyone should arrive in New York like this – at least once in a lifetime.' And we have only one lifetime.

When, heading towards that unforgettable experience for the first time, I made my dramatic exit from the London advertizing agency, one of the friends and colleagues I reluctantly left behind was a sparky, black-haired young Austrian-born woman who, with great charm and efficiency, ran the PR department (including a model kitchen in which were evolved and tested the recipes used in our campaigns for such products as Guinness, Colman and Bovril) and was already starting her career as a food writer, for *Vogue*. Her name was Gretel Beer, and she too has evolved with the years. She achieved fame as the distinguished food and travel writer of the *Daily Telegraph* and of the *Sunday Express* in its heyday under the editorship of the legendary John Junor. In 1954 she published her definitive *Austrian Cooking* – the first of almost a dozen cookbooks – and it has never since been out of print. She has remained my friend to this day and, natural bias apart, it would be hard to think of anyone better qualified – as seasoned traveller, skilled cook and wise observer of the world's ways – to bring into your home, in easy-to-follow form, the glories of the QE2's cuisine. *Bon voyage* on your journey of discovery, and *bon appétit!*

9

# Soup
## of the evening,
## beautiful soup

Soups have always featured prominently in the culinary repertoire of the QE2 – in the old days you could even start the day with French onion soup which was on the breakfast menu, together with lamb chops! On one occasion I was witness to these being ordered – and consumed with great gusto – by a fellow passenger who was a Swiss banker. The accompanying salad of grated radishes was not on the menu, but was produced without a murmur or a raising of the eyebrow – just part of the impeccable QE2 service.

French onion soup is still featured on the QE2's menu, but there is now a much greater selection of soups and a daily choice of three different types for every meal. Some are gently soothing like the Fennel Velouté with Poached Scallops or the Clam Chowder, others are more robust like the Black Bean Soup with Coriander Cream or deeply traditional like Chef Brian Scott's Cock-a-Leekie to which Thierry Guimard has added a Gallic touch of tarragon. Or there's the strong and spicy Gulyas Soup which could take pride of place in any Hungarian restaurant.

Clear consommé – beef as well as chicken – is always on the menu. About seventy pounds of fresh beef and twenty pints of egg white are used daily for clarifying the beef consommé alone. It is strong, pungent – redolent of the famous Olio soup presented at Court balls in Imperial Vienna and often served with sliced wood mushrooms or turned into Stracciatelle alla Romana or – the Austrian influence again – with small liver dumplings or semolina gnocchi.

There is a great repertoire of cold soups as well – unusual combinations such as Watercress Soup with Smoked Trout and wonderful cold fruit soups practically spanning the globe in their origin – some made with sparkling wine or 'spirited' with Aquavit.

TRICOLORE SOUP OF PEPPERS

# · Soups ·

Pumpkin Soup

Cream of Courgettes and Mushrooms

Cream of Lentil Soup

Cream of Herb Soup

Clam Chowder

Gulyas Soup

Cock-a-Leekie

Black Bean Soup with Coriander Cream

Tricolore Soup of Peppers

Tomato Soup
with Basil Cream

Fennel Velouté with Poached Scallops

Stracciatelle alla Romana

Semolina Gnocchi

Small Liver Dumplings

Chilled Watercress Soup
with Smoked Trout

Chilled Cucumber Soup

Chilled Roasted White Peach Soup

Chilled Pear, Nectarine or Apple Soup
with Sparkling Wine

Chilled Cantaloupe Soup

Chilled Cranberry Soup with Aquavit

Chilled Grape Soup

Chilled Coconut Soup with Lime

Chilled Three-Melon Soup

Chilled Honeydew Melon Soup

Chilled Pina Colada Soup

# Pumpkin Soup

Serves 5–6

60g (2oz) onion, *finely chopped*
½ garlic clove, *finely chopped*
15g (½oz) butter
450g (1lb) pumpkin, *seeded, peeled and*
  *roughly chopped*
225g (8oz) carrots, *peeled and sliced*
1 litre (1¾ pint) chicken stock
110ml (4fl oz) double cream
salt and pepper
1 tablespoon roasted pumpkin seeds,
  *green pumpkin-seed oil (optional), to serve*

Sauté onion and garlic in butter. Add pumpkin, carrots and soften them gently with the onions and garlic. Cover with chicken stock and cook until carrots are soft – about thirty minutes. Place in a blender or food processor with the cream and blend until smooth. Return the soup to the saucepan and reheat gently. Season with salt and pepper. Serve sprinkled with toasted pumpkin seeds and – if possible – with a little green pumpkin-seed oil swirled into each serving.

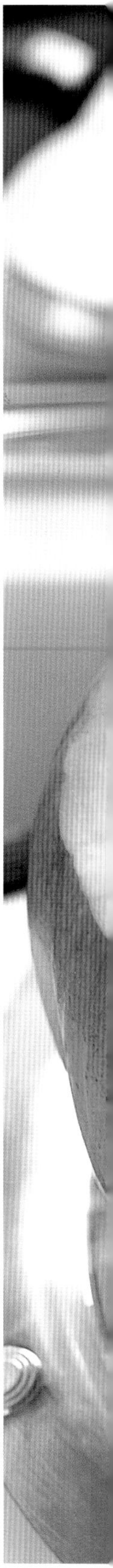

QE2

## Cream of Courgettes and Mushrooms

**Serves 4**

*1 small onion, chopped*
*450g (1lb) mushrooms*
*200g (7oz) courgettes*
*2 tablespoons butter*
*1 scant tablespoon flour*
*500ml (18fl oz) milk*
*500ml (18fl oz) chicken stock*
*2 teaspoons salt*
*1 teaspoon pepper*
*1 tablespoon chopped herbs*

Sauté onion, mushrooms and sliced courgettes in one tablespoon butter until soft. Blend remaining butter with the flour. Purée vegetables in a food processor until smooth. Return purée to rinsed-out saucepan, add milk and stock and bring to boil. Add the butter/flour mixture in small flakes and simmer, stirring constantly, until well-blended. Season with salt and pepper.

Serve sprinkled with chopped herbs.

## Cream of Lentil Soup

**Serves 4**

*100g (4oz) streaky bacon*
*50g (2oz) butter*
*100g (4oz) onions, chopped*
*1 garlic clove, crushed*
*500g (1lb 2oz) brown lentils, soaked overnight*
*400ml (16fl oz) chicken stock*
*200ml (8fl oz) double cream*
*2 teaspoons salt*
*1 teaspoon pepper*
*2 tablespoons chopped parsley*

Dice the bacon. Fry the bacon lightly in the butter, then add onions and garlic and sauté until translucent. Add drained and rinsed lentils together with the stock, and cook until lentils are soft. Blend in a food processor, sieve and return to rinsed-out saucepan to reheat. Add cream and seasoning.

Serve sprinkled with chopped parsley.

## Cream of Herb Soup

**Serves 4**

*100g (3½oz) onion, chopped*
*50g (2oz) butter*
*50g (2oz) flour*
*500ml (18fl oz) chicken stock*
*500ml (18fl oz) milk*
*5 tablespoons chopped parsley*
*5 tablespoons chopped basil*
*5 tablespoons chopped marjoram*
*2 tablespoons chopped sage*
*salt and pepper*
*croutons for garnish*

Sweat the onion in the butter without colouring. Stir in the flour and add the chicken stock slowly, stirring all the time so that there are no lumps. Gradually add the milk. Simmer gently for twenty minutes until well-blended. Add all the herbs at the last minute and process. Adjust seasoning with salt and pepper.

Serve with croutons.

# Clam Chowder

## Serves 10

280g (10oz) diced salt pork
50g (2oz) butter
1 large onion, finely chopped
100g (3½oz) diced celery
5 medium sized potatoes, peeled and diced
600ml (21½ fl oz) clam juice
600ml (21½ fl oz) water
1 teaspoon chopped thyme
white pepper
1 litre (1¾ pints) milk
1 litre (1¾ pints) single cream
500g (18oz) large clams
salt
chopped parsley for garnish

In a thick-bottomed pan, brown the salt pork in its own fat until crisp. Remove from pan and keep warm. Add butter to the rendered fat and sauté onions and celery until softened. Add potatoes, clam juice, water, thyme and salt pork and pepper. Simmer uncovered until potatoes are tender. Stir in milk, cream and clams. Heat through, but do not boil and adjust seasoning, adding salt if necessary. Garnish with chopped parsley.

# Gulyas Soup

## 8 servings

900g (2lb) onions, finely chopped
3 garlic cloves, crushed
4 tablespoons oil or pork dripping
1 tablespoon wine vinegar
3 tablespoons sweet Hungarian paprika
1 tablespoon tomato paste
salt and pepper
2 litres (3½ pints) beef stock or water
900g (2lb) beef, diced
3 large potatoes cut into small cubes
1 tablespoon flour
1 teaspoon ground caraway seeds
2 teaspoons chopped marjoram
A little grated lemon rind

Sauté the onions in oil or pork dripping until golden brown, add crushed garlic cloves and stir, then add vinegar, paprika and tomato paste and stir together over low heat, being careful not to burn the paprika. Add seasoning and the stock (or water) and bring to simmering point, then add meat. Simmer gently until the meat is nearly cooked, skimming off any impurities – but not the fat – rising to the surface, then add potatoes and simmer until potatoes and meat are cooked.

Thicken the soup by stirring the flour into a little of the fat skimmed off the top and add it in small flakes to the liquid. Cook for another few minutes for the soup to thicken. Taste and adjust seasoning if necessary. 'If you like a hotter taste,' says Karl Winkler, 'add a pinch of chilli or some hot paprika – sold as rose paprika.'

Serve with fresh rye bread or crisp white rolls.

QE2

# Cock-a-Leekie

**Serves 6**

*450g (1lb) chicken bones, wing tips etc., chopped*
*1 tablespoon olive oil*
*1 carrot*
*1 onion*
*2 leeks*
*2 celery stalks*
*2¼ litres (4 pints) water*
*2 tablespoons chicken bouillon powder*
*salt and pepper*
*2 chicken breasts*
*½ bunch tarragon*
*6 prunes, soaked, stones removed and sliced*
*4 tablespoons long-grain rice, cooked*

Lightly brown the chicken bones in olive oil. Add carrot, onion, one leek and the celery and sweat together, then add the water and the bouillon powder. Bring to the boil and simmer until liquid is reduced by half. Strain and reduce by another quarter. Adjust seasoning if necessary. Flatten the chicken breasts and spread out on clingfilm. Roll up each chicken breast with tarragon in the centre. Secure ends of film tightly and poach chicken breasts for six to eight minutes. Cut remaining leek into julienne strips and poach in the chicken broth. Remove film and cut chicken breasts into rounds. Add to soup, together with prunes, and rice.

SOUP OF THE EVENING, BEAUTIFUL SOUP

QE2

# Black Bean Soup with Coriander Cream

### Serves 6–8

*1 onion, diced*
*5 rashers bacon*
*2 cloves garlic, chopped*
*1 carrot, diced*
*2 tomatoes, chopped*
*1 red pepper, chopped*
*1 yellow pepper, chopped*
*¼ habanero pepper (mild chilli pepper), chopped*
*2 cups  black beans, soaked overnight in water*
*1½ litres (2¾ pints) chicken stock*
*¼ cup tomato paste*
*½ bunch coriander*
*2 sprigs thyme*
*1 teaspoon ground cumin*
*salt and pepper*
*juice of 1 lemon*

### Garnish

*¼ bunch of coriander*
*1 cup sour cream*
*salt and pepper*
*1 teaspoon lemon juice*
*1 red onion, finely chopped*

Dice the bacon and fry in its own fat until browned and crisp. Add onion, garlic, carrot, tomatoes, red and yellow peppers and habanero pepper. Sauté until the vegetables are soft. Add the drained black beans, chicken stock, tomato paste, coriander, thyme and cumin and stir. Simmer until the black beans are soft, about one to one and a half hours. Remove from heat and cool for five to ten minutes, then blend in a mixer or food processor until smooth. Sieve into the rinsed out saucepan, adjust seasoning with salt and pepper and simmer for another five to ten minutes. Add lemon juice.

To make the coriander cream, process the coriander with one tablespoon water to a smooth purée. Fold into the sour cream and season with salt and pepper and lemon juice.

Serve soup in warmed bowls with a swirl of coriander cream and finely chopped red onion.

# Tricolore Soup of Peppers

ILLUSTRATED ON PAGE 10

### Serves 6

*5 red peppers, seeded and diced*
*5 yellow peppers, seeded and diced*
*5 green peppers, seeded and diced*
*3 tablespoons olive oil*
*1 onion, peeled and diced*
*2 litres (3½ pints) vegetable bouillon*
*salt*
*Tabasco sauce*

Sauté each colour of peppers separately, in separate saucepans, in a tablespoon of olive oil. Add a third of the chopped onion to each lot of peppers and sauté until onions are translucent. Pour in a third of the vegetable bouillon to each lot of peppers and simmer until peppers are soft. Process each lot separately until smooth, then sieve and season with salt and Tabasco sauce. Reheat gently and pour each colour separately into soup plates to achieve tricolore effect.

# Tomato Soup
# with Basil Cream

## Serves 6

*1 onion, chopped*
*1 carrot, diced*
*2 cloves garlic, crushed*
*3 tablespoons olive oil*
*4 tomatoes*
*2 tins 400g (14oz) plum tomatoes*
*560ml (1 pint) chicken stock*
*1 teaspoon chopped oregano*
*1 bay leaf*
*parsley stalks*
*140ml (¼ pint) double cream*
*salt and pepper*
*1 tablespoon sugar*
*12 fresh basil leaves*

Sauté onion, carrot and garlic in olive oil, add tomatoes, stock and herbs, except for the basil. Add sugar. Cook gently for ten minutes, remove bay leaf then blend in a mixer and sieve. Blend basil in a mixer or food processor with the cream. Reheat soup gently, adjust seasoning with salt and pepper and sugar if necessary. Pour soup into plates or bowls and garnish with a swirl of the basil cream.

# Fennel Velouté with
# Poached Scallops

## Serves 4

*500ml (18fl oz) fish stock*
*500g (18oz) fennel, diced*
*4 shallots, chopped*
*50ml (2fl oz) olive oil*
*1 tablespoon flour*
*½ cup white wine*
*2 tablespoons Pernod*
*4 tablespoons Noilly Prat*
*1 tablespoon chopped chervil*
*125ml (4½ fl oz) double cream*
*2 tablespoons butter*
*12 scallops*
*4 sprigs fresh chervil for garnish*
*salt and pepper*

Set aside a little of the fish stock for poaching the scallops. Sauté the fennel and shallots in the olive oil for five minutes, then add the flour and continue stirring over low heat for a further two minutes. Add the white wine, Pernod and Noilly Prat and bring to simmering point while stirring, then add the fish stock and simmer slowly for half an hour.

Blend the soup in a food processor with the chopped chervil and strain through a fine sieve. Add the double cream, seasoning and adjust the thickness if necessary: if too thin bring back to simmering point to reduce; if too thick add more stock. Take the soup off the heat and whisk in the butter.

Poach the scallops for two minutes in the reserved fish stock and place three scallops in each soup plate. Pour soup over the scallops and garnish with chervil sprigs.

# Stracciatelle alla Romana

Serves 6

*3 eggs*
*45g (1½ oz) grated Parmesan cheese*
*15g (½ oz) semolina or strong flour*
*salt, white pepper and nutmeg*
*1⅛ litres (2 pints) beef or chicken broth*
*2 tablespoons finely chopped chives or parsley*

Combine the eggs, Parmesan, semolina or flour, salt and white pepper and nutmeg in a mixing bowl. Beat lightly. Bring the broth to simmering point, then pour egg mixture into the broth in a steady stream, stirring to break up any lumps, but not stirring too briskly. Allow to simmer for thirty seconds and remove from heat. Serve sprinkled with the chives or parsley.

# Semolina Gnocchi

(for clear consommé)

*1 heaped tablespoon butter*
*salt*
*11 heaped teaspoons coarse semolina*
*1 egg*

Cream butter with a pinch salt, beat in half the semolina, then the egg and finally the remaining semolina. Cover and leave to stand for one hour. Scoop out small portions with a spoon and drop into boiling broth. Lower heat and simmer for eight to ten minutes, until gnocchi rise to the top. Alternatively cook the gnocchi in a large pan of slightly salted water, fish them out with a slotted spoon when they rise to the top and add them to the soup.

# Small Liver Dumplings

(for clear consommé)

*2 bread rolls (day old)*
*1 small onion or shallot*
*180g (6oz) pig's or calf's liver*
*30g (1oz) butter or lard*
*chopped parsley and marjoram*
*1 tablespoon plain flour*
*60g (2oz) fine fresh breadcrumbs*
*1 egg*
*salt and pepper*

Grate the crust off the rolls, then break or cut up the rolls coarsely and soak in water to soften. Chop the onion or shallot finely. Mince the liver, then squeeze out all the moisture from the rolls and mince them as well. Melt butter or lard, fry onion or shallot very lightly to soften. Add the minced rolls, stir once to blend and remove from heat. Add parsley and marjoram, liver, flour, breadcrumbs and egg. Season with salt and pepper. Mix everything well, then set aside for fifteen to twenty minutes.

Form a small dumpling, about 2½ cm (1in) and drop into boiling beef broth, lower heat and simmer with the lid tilted for about fifteen minutes, Test the dumpling: if the mixture is too soft, add a little extra flour or breadcrumbs, if too dry, add a little milk to the remaining mixture. Shape into small dumplings and cook as described.

# Chilled Watercress Soup with Smoked Trout

ILLUSTRATED ON PAGE 22

Serves 4

*100g (3½ oz) onions, chopped*
*2 tablespoons olive oil*
*1 litre (1¾ pints) chicken stock*
*1 clove garlic, halved*
*1 cup double cream*
*250g (9oz) watercress, cleaned*
*salt and pepper*
*½ cup yoghurt*
*1 smoked trout fillet*

Sauté onions in olive oil. Add chicken stock, garlic, cream and watercress stems. Simmer for twenty minutes. Blend in mixer or food processor and sieve. Add the watercress leaves, reserving a few for decoration and simmer for five minutes. Blend in mixer or food processor and simmer until creamy. Season with salt and pepper. Chill for at least two hours. Serve in soup plates with a swirl of yoghurt, some flaked smoked trout fillet and a few watercress leaves.

# Chilled Cucumber Soup

Serves 6

*4 medium cucumbers, peeled and seeded*
*½ cup single cream*
*2 cups plain yoghurt*
*2 cups sour cream*
*pinch salt*
*white pepper*
*2 teaspoons chopped fresh dill*

Cut cucumber into chunks and blend with single cream, yoghurt and sour cream. Season with salt and white pepper. Chill well and serve garnished with chopped dill.

THE · QUEEN'S · GRILL

*The Queen's Grill – now the most exclusive restaurant on board the QE2 – was originally a discotheque where Ringo Starr and George Harrison gave impromptu performances during a 1969 Transatlantic Crossing.*

CHILLED WATERCRESS SOUP WITH SMOKED TROUT

# Chilled Roasted White Peach Soup

### Serves 4

*6 ripe white peaches, peeled, halved and stoned*
*1½ cups granulated sugar*
*2 cups water*
*vanilla pod, split*
*star anise, cracked*
*juice 3 oranges*
*juice 2 lemons*
*2–3 tablespoons double cream (optional)*
*280ml (½ pint) wild strawberries, washed and*
*    dried*
*4 fresh mint sprigs*

Preheat the oven to 200°C / 400°F / Gas 6. Lightly coat a baking sheet with butter. Place the peach halves on the prepared baking sheet, cut side down. Sprinkle the peaches with half cup of the sugar and bake for fifteen to twenty minutes, until well roasted.

Transfer the peaches to a food processor, together with any juice from the baking sheet. Purée until smooth, stopping two or three times to scrape down the sides. Transfer to a large bowl and set aside.

Combine water and remaining sugar in a small saucepan, together with the vanilla pod and the star anise. Bring to boil slowly and remove from heat. Leave to infuse for about one hour in a warm place. Strain through a fine sieve and add orange and lemon juices. Slowly add the citrus syrup to the peach purée, tasting as you go, until the desired consistency and flavour is reached. If it tastes right, but appears to be too thick, thin it down with a little water or cream. Cover and chill before serving.

To serve, ladle the soup into chilled soup plates and garnish with the strawberries and the mint sprigs.

# Chilled Pear, Nectarine or Apple Soup with Sparkling Wine

### Serves 8

*900g (2lb) pears, nectarines or apples, peeled,*
*    cored or stoned*
*560ml (1 pint) water*
*about ½ cup sugar, depending on acidity of fruit*
*2 cinnamon sticks*
*5 cloves*
*a few strips of lemon peel and juice 1 lemon*
*750ml (27fl oz) sparkling white wine*
*60ml (2fl oz) Pear William, peach liqueur  or*
*    Calvados (according to fruit)*

Retain a little of the fruit and dice it for garnishing. Simmer remaining fruit with the water, sugar, spices and lemon peel and juice slowly for five minutes or until the fruit is soft. Remove cinnamon sticks, cloves and lemon rind and process fruit and liquid until smooth. Leave to cool and chill well. Add chilled sparkling wine and liqueur and garnish with diced fruit.

QE2

# Chilled Cantaloupe Soup

**Serves 6**

*2 cups orange juice*
*2 cups apple juice*
*1 cup dry white wine*
*2 tablespoons tapioca*
*1 ripe medium cantaloupe melon*
*salt*
*cayenne pepper*
*sprigs of fresh mint*

Combine orange juice, apple juice, dry white wine and tapioca in a saucepan and simmer gently over medium heat for ten minutes. Allow mixture to cool and then chill. Cut melon in half, removing seeds and scoop out the flesh. Divide flesh into two equal portions, coarsely chopping one and finely dicing the other. Put coarsely chopped melon into blender or food processor with one cup of the chilled juice mixture and purée until smooth. Pour purée into a mixing bowl and add remainder of chilled juice and finely diced melon. Adjust seasoning with salt and a touch of cayenne.

Serve cold in a cup set in a bed of crushed ice, decorated with a sprig of fresh mint. Or serve in one half of of a cantaloupe with enough flesh scooped out to hold the soup.

SOUP OF THE EVENING, BEAUTIFUL SOUP

QE2

(FROM TOP, CLOCKWISE)
CHILLED GRAPE SOUP,
CHILLED COCONUT SOUP WITH LIME,
CHILLED NECTARINE SOUP WITH SPARKLING WINE,
CHILLED CRANBERRY SOUP WITH AQUAVIT,
CHILLED HONEYDEW MELON SOUP.

# Chilled Cranberry Soup with Aquavit

ILLUSTRATED ON PREVIOUS PAGE

**Serves 4**

*2 cups cranberries, fresh or frozen*
*¼ stick cinnamon*
*1 cup red wine*
*1 cup water*
*½ cup sugar*
*½ tablespoon lemon juice*
*3 tablespoons Aquavit*
*1 cup vanilla ice-cream*

Cook the cranberries with cinnamon, red wine, water and sugar for about fifteen minutes. Add lemon juice and remove the cinnamon. Blend for a few minutes. Strain the soup into a bowl and set on crushed ice to cool. Chill in refrigerator for one hour and just before serving pour in the Aquavit and swirl in the ice-cream.

# Chilled Coconut Soup with Lime

ILLUSTRATED ON PREVIOUS PAGE

**Serves 4**

*2 cups lime sorbet (see page 50)*
*1 tablespoon brown rum*
*1 cup single cream*
*1 cup unsweetened coconut milk*
*1 teaspoon lime juice*
*2 tablespoons toasted coconut*
*mint leaves for decoration*

Combine lime sorbet, rum, cream, coconut milk and lime juice. Blend in a food processor. Pour mixture into soup cups, garnish with toasted coconut and mint leaves and serve at once.

# Chilled Grape Soup

ILLUSTRATED ON PREVIOUS PAGE

**Serves 4**

*3 cups seedless black grapes*
*1 teaspoon lemon juice*
*2 cups low fat yoghurt*
*½ cup soda water*
*fresh mint leaves for garnish*

Combine all ingredients except the soda water and mint leaves and blend in a food processor until smooth. Chill for a few hours. Just before serving, add the soda water and stir to mix. Serve garnished with mint leaves.

QE2

# Chilled Three-Melon Soup

### Serves 6–8

*250ml (9fl oz) sugar syrup (see page 50)*
*star anise, grated lemon and orange rind,*
*    cardamom*
*1 cantaloupe melon*
*1 honeydew melon*
*½ watermelon*
*1 litre (1¾ pints) mineral water*
*500ml (18fl oz) sparkling white wine*
*125ml (4½fl oz) Medori liqueur*
*juice 2 lemons*
*sprigs of mint*

Make an infusion with the sugar syrup, star anise, grated lemon and orange rind and cardamom. Scoop out melon flesh and cut part into small cubes for garnish. Put remaining melon flesh into food processor, together with all the other ingredients, except sugar syrup and process until smooth. Strain in the sugar syrup and stir to mix. Chill before serving, decorated with mint sprigs.

# Chilled Honeydew Melon Soup

### Serves 4

*1 honeydew melon weighing about 2lb (900g)*
*juice of 1 lemon*
*½ cup simple sugar syrup (see page 50)*
*lemon slices*
*sprigs of mint*

Halve melon and remove seeds. Scoop out four small rounds with a melon baller, moisten with a little of the lemon juice and chill. Cut remaining melon flesh into chunks and put into a blender. Add lemon juice and sweeten to taste with the sugar syrup. Chill for two hours.

Serve garnished with reserved melon balls, some lemon slices and sprigs of mint.

# Chilled Pina Colada Soup

### Serves 4–6

*650g (23 oz) pineapple*
*400g (14 oz) coconut ice-cream*
*3 tablespoons Meyers rum*
*600ml (21½ fl oz) milk*

Peel pineapple, remove hard core, dice and process with all the other ingredients.
Serve at once.

QE2

# Caviar, morning, noon and night

Since Cunard is the world's largest consumer of caviar, one might be forgiven for thinking that QE2 passengers started and ended their days on board with this delicacy. It would be perfectly possible, of course. Start with shirred eggs and caviar for breakfast – or ask for a dollop of caviar on your Eggs Benedict – though these are normally topped with a sliver of truffle – have snacks such as potatoes stuffed with crème fraîche and caviar – caviar as hors d'oeuvre at main meals and the odd caviar canapé in between.

But it would mean missing out on some of the best QE2 starters. Superb Shellfish Terrine and Moules Poulette, specialities of Chef de Cuisine Thierry Guimard, a native of Nantes where – as he points out – 'beurre blanc was invented' (by a woman, incidentally) which is often incorporated in his recipes. Beefsteak Tartare is another QE2 special, as is their way of preparing Gravad Lax.

Some of the starters are quite substantial though they may not look it – like Goose-liver Medallions seared with fresh peaches and flambéed at the table with peach eau-de-vie (calling perhaps for one of the calorie-restricted main courses from the Spa menu to follow). Or you could get the best of all worlds and order a Napoleon of Smoked Salmon: layers of smoked salmon, hardboiled egg yolk, crème fraîche – and caviar!

NAPOLEON OF SMOKED SALMON WITH CAVIAR

## · Starters and Snacks ·

Eggs Benedict with Smoked Salmon

Snail Puffs

Salmon Tartare with Yoghurt Dill Sauce

Avocado and Smoked Salmon Mousse
with Basil and Spring Onion Vinaigrette

Fried Eggs Sailor Style

Gravad Lax with Mustard and Dill
Sauce

Moules Poulette

Napoleon of Smoked Salmon
with Caviar

Crab and Lobster Cakes
with Potato Crust, Fondue of Fennel
and Bouillabaisse Jus

Crown of Scallops and New Potatoes
with Saffron Vinaigrette

Rillet of Salmon
with Crayfish and Cucumber

Shellfish Terrine

Braised Oxtail Salad
with Tomato Chutney

Marinated Beef Fillet
with Herbs

Goose-liver Medallions
with Poached Peaches

# Eggs Benedict with Smoked Salmon

### Serves 4

*4 eggs*
*2 English muffins*
*4 slices smoked salmon*
*4 small truffle slices*
*salt*
*wine vinegar*

## Sauce Hollandaise

*2 egg yolks*
*125g (4½oz) clarified butter*
*salt and pepper*
*cayenne pepper*
*1 tablespoon lemon juice*

Poach the eggs in lightly vinegared water and place into warm salted water. Prepare the Hollandaise by putting the egg yolks in a small saucepan or bowl and adding two teaspoons cold water. Heat very slowly, whisking all the time until frothy and each movement of the whisk shows the bottom of the saucepan. (If using a bowl, suspend it over a saucepan of barely simmering water.) Add slightly warm clarified butter little by little until fully incorporated. Season with salt and pepper, cayenne pepper and lemon juice.

Split the muffins in half and toast. Place smoked salmon slices on top of each muffin half. Take eggs out of water and dry on a paper towel. Place on top of salmon and glaze with Hollandaise Sauce. Garnish with a truffle slice.

QE2

# Snail Puffs

**Makes 24**

8 tablespoons butter
24 snails (tinned)
6 shallots, finely chopped
120g (4½oz) chopped mushrooms
2 tablespoons brandy
salt and pepper
grated nutmeg
chopped fresh thyme
1 clove garlic, crushed
120g (4½oz) chopped walnuts
2 tablespoons chopped parsley
1 tablespoon lemon juice
125ml (4½fl oz) dry white wine

## Batter

2 egg yolks
300g (11oz) flour
300ml (11fl oz) beer or white wine
salt
50ml (2fl oz) olive oil
3 egg whites
oil for deep-frying

Heat half the butter in a frying pan and lightly sauté snails, shallots and mushrooms. Add brandy and flame. Remove from heat. Season with salt and pepper, nutmeg and thyme. Mix in garlic, walnuts, parsley, lemon juice and white wine. Blend well and chill for two hours. Cream remaining butter until fluffy and blend into snail mixture. Chill until use.

For the batter, whisk together egg yolks, flour and beer (or dry white wine) with a pinch of salt, fold in the olive oil. Whisk egg whites until stiff. Heat oil to 180°C/350°F. Fold whisked egg whites into batter mixture. Scoop out portions of the chilled snail mixture, dip into batter and deep fry. Drain on kitchen paper and serve at once.

# Salmon Tartare with Yoghurt Dill Sauce

**Serves 2**

## Salmon Tartare

500g (18oz) salmon piece, cut from the tail,
        skinned and cut into small chunks
2 tablespoons olive oil
1 tablespoon lemon juice
1½ tablespoons mixed chopped fresh herbs
        (parsley, thyme, chervil)
1 tablespoon finely chopped shallots
salt and black pepper
½ avocado pear, pitted and sliced

## Yoghurt Dill Sauce

30ml (1fl oz) sour cream
30ml (1fl oz) yoghurt
1 tablespoon lemon juice
1 tablespoon of chopped dill
salt and freshly ground black pepper
red peppercorns to garnish

To make the sauce, combine all ingredients, except the red peppercorns and refrigerate until required. Combine salmon, olive oil, lemon juice, herbs and shallots on a cutting board. Season with salt and freshly ground black pepper. Using a large knife, finely chop the salmon, herbs and shallots until you have a tartare mixture. Transfer to a bowl and stir to combine. Form the mixture into patties, filling a pastry cutter for easier handling. Place patties on each plate and surround with an avocado fan. Spoon sauce on the side and sprinkle with red peppercorns. Serve immediately.

# Avocado and Smoked Salmon Mousse with Basil and Spring Onion Vinaigrette

## Serves 6

250g (9oz) smoked salmon, sliced
3 avocado pears
juice 1 lemon
pinch of salt and cayenne pepper
90ml (3fl oz) double cream, whipped

## Vinaigrette

60g (2oz) basil leaves
2 spring onion stalks
110ml (4fl oz) cider vinegar
90ml (3fl oz) sunflower oil
salt and pepper
cucumber, lemon and fresh sprigs of dill for garnish
small salad leaves

Line six very lightly oiled ramekins with the smoked salmon, leaving enough salmon overlapping to completely cover the mousse after filling. Purée the avocado in a blender or food processor, add the lemon juice and seasoning. Fold in the whipped cream. Spoon the mixture into the salmon-lined ramekins and cover with the overlapping salmon. Refrigerate for two hours before serving.

To make the vinaigrette, purée the basil and spring onion with the vinegar and salt and pepper until smooth, then slowly add the sunflower oil.

To serve, arrange a ring of finely sliced seedless cucumber on each plate and place chilled mousse in centre. Top each one with a thin skinless slice of lemon and a sprig of dill.

Dress plate around mousse with small salad leaves (lambs lettuce is ideal) and sprinkle with the vinaigrette.

# Fried Eggs Sailor Style

## Serves 2

4 tablespoons butter
1 small onion, chopped
1 tablespoon brandy
½ cup double cream
200g (7oz) cooked and shelled prawns
salt and pepper
4 eggs
dill sprigs for garnish

Heat half the butter in a frying pan, add chopped onion and sauté until lightly browned. Add brandy and cream, stirring to scrape up any browned bits from the bottom of the pan. Simmer until reduced by half. Add prawns, season with salt and pepper and keep warm. Heat remaining butter in another frying pan and fry eggs over low heat until yolks have set.

Arrange prawn mixture on warm plates and place fried eggs on top. Garnish with dill.

QE2

# Gravad Lax with Mustard and Dill Sauce

**20 portions**

*2 sides fresh salmon, scaled and boned,
     with the skin left on*
*½ cup coarse salt*
*1 cup caster sugar*
*1 tablespoon white peppercorns, crushed*
*1 teaspoon juniper berries, crushed*
*1 teaspoon fennel seeds, crushed*
*1 bunch fresh dill, chopped*
*2 tablespoons Dijon or Swedish mustard*
*freshly chopped dill for finishing*

Wash salmon sides and pat dry with a paper towel. Place sides in a tray, skin side down. Mix together salt, sugar and crushed spices and sprinkle over fish. Sprinkle chopped dill over one side of the salmon and place other side of salmon on top, skin side up. Cover with foil and weigh down with a board. Refrigerate for three days, turning the fish over daily.

Take the fish out of the brine which will have formed and gently scrape off dill. Spread cut sides of the fish with mustard and sprinkle with freshly chopped dill. Place salmon, skin side down on a cutting board and slice, on the slant, as thinly as possible. Serve on chilled plates with mustard and dill sauce, sliced cucumber and lemon wedges.

## Mustard and Dill Sauce

*1 cup salad oil*
*3 tablespoons mild mustard*
*2 tablespoons wine vinegar*
*3 tablespoons sugar*
*salt and white pepper*
*2 tablespoons chopped dill*

Whisk the oil gradually into the mustard, adding the vinegar slowly. Season with sugar and salt and white pepper and chopped dill.

GRAVAD LAX
WITH MUSTARD
AND DILL SAUCE

QE2

# Moules Poulette

Serves 4

2kg (4½ lb) mussels
bunch of parsley
200g (7oz) finely chopped shallots
2 heaped tablespoons butter
1 lightly heaped tablespoon flour
250ml (9fl oz) dry white wine
250ml (9fl oz) double cream
salt and pepper
1 French baguette, sliced
50g (2oz) butter
1 tablespoon chopped parsley
2 garlic cloves, crushed

Clean, wash and scrape the mussels. Throw away
any that do not close when tapped sharply. Sweat
the shallots in one tablespoon of the butter.
Work flour into remaining tablespoon of butter
and set aside. Add mussels and wine to the
shallots and cook for about eight minutes,
shaking the saucepan gently from time to time.
Remove mussels from saucepan and throw away
any that have not opened. Reduce juice in
saucepan a little, add cream and stir in the
flour/butter mixture in small flakes. Return
mussels to saucepan and serve sprinkled with
chopped parsley, seasoning and herbed bread
made by cutting the baguette into slices and
spreading with creamed butter, parsley and
crushed garlic mixture and baking in a hot oven
(220°C/425°F/Gas 7) for about twelve minutes.

# Napoleon of Smoked Salmon with Caviar

ILLUSTRATED ON PAGE 28

Serves 4

12 slices smoked salmon
4 eggs
1 bottle (375ml/13½ fl oz) balsamic vinegar
2 bunches chives
½ cup sour cream
4 tablespoons caviar
4 small salad bouquets (small salad leaves)
4 onion rings
3-4 tablespoons vinaigrette (see page 45)

Dice the smoked salmon. Boil the eggs for twelve
minutes. Rinse eggs under cold tap, shell and
halve. Separate egg yolks from whites and chop
the yolks very finely and chill. (The whites are
not used.) Pour the balsamic vinegar into a small
saucepan and reduce to one third, then pour into
a small jug. Chop the chives finely or snip with
scissors.

Place a pastry cutter 5cm (2in) diameter and
7½ cm (3in) high on each plate and fill with a
layer of diced, smoked salmon. The next layer is
chopped chives, then the egg yolk, sour cream
and another layer of smoked salmon. Top with
caviar.

Thread each salad bouquet through an onion
ring and place next to the Napoleon sprinkle with
vinaigrette. Remove pastry cutter and garnish
plate with the balsamic vinegar.

QE2

# Crab and Lobster Cakes with Potato Crust, Fondue of Fennel and Bouillabaisse Jus

QE2

**Serves 4**

200g (7oz) fresh crab, flaked

200g (7oz) lobster tail, diced

1 stick celery, diced

1 red pepper, diced

1 green pepper, diced

100g (3½oz) white bread, crusts removed, cubed

2 eggs

1 tablespoon mayonnaise

salt and pepper

2 potatoes, julienne cut

oil for frying

1 mango, diced

## Fennel Fondue

2 fennel bulbs

butter

250ml (9fl oz) white wine

150ml (5½fl oz) double cream

## Bouillabaisse Jus

1 onion, sliced

1 carrot, sliced

½ leek, sliced

1 fennel bulb, sliced

2 cloves garlic

1 teaspoon butter

salt and pepper

1 teaspoon tomato paste

3 cloves

2 bay leaves

saffron threads

100ml (3½fl oz) Pernod

100ml (3½fl oz) white wine

250ml (9fl oz) fish stock

2 tablespoons lobster butter

In a mixing bowl combine crab flakes, diced lobster, diced celery, red and green peppers, cubed bread, eggs and mayonnaise. Season.

Form into four round cakes and cover with julienne strips of potato. Fry in hot oil on both sides and keep warm.

For the fondue of fennel, slice the fennel bulbs finely and sauté in a little butter until soft. Add white wine and reduce completely, then add cream and reduce until thickened.

Arrange cakes on plates and surround with portions of fennel fondue and diced mango pieces.

For the jus, lightly sauté the vegetables in the butter, add seasoning, tomato paste and spices. Pour in the Pernod and white wine and reduce to half, then add fish stock and cook for thirty minutes to reduce again. Strain and finish with butter. Sprinkle jus over crab cakes.

CRAB AND LOBSTER CAKES
WITH POTATO CRUST, FONDUE OF FENNEL
AND BOUILLABAISSE JUS

# Crown of Scallops and New Potatoes with Saffron Vinaigrette

**Serves 4**

450g (1lb) scallops, without the coral

6 small new potatoes

5 tablespoons olive oil

1 teaspoon chopped thyme

2 cups aromatic salad (arrugula, lambs lettuce,
    basil, tarragon, chervil, flat-leaf parsley,
    watercress)

1 tablespoon balsamic vinegar

salt and pepper

1 artichoke, trimmed

16 slices of black truffle

balsamic vinegar for garnish

butter for the plate

## Saffron Vinaigrette

50g (2oz) finely chopped shallots

¼ cup finely chopped fennel

1 clove garlic, crushed

2 tablespoons olive oil

1 tablespoon Noilly Prat

2 cups white wine

2 tablespoons truffle juice

pinch saffron

500ml (18fl oz) double cream

2 tablespoons oyster or clam juice

1 tablespoon cornflour slaked with 2 tablespoons
    water

¼ cup walnut oil

½ teaspoon white wine or tarragon vinegar

salt and pepper

For the dressing, sauté shallots, fennel and garlic in olive oil until translucent. Add Noilly Prat and white wine, reduce until liquid has evaporated. Add truffle juice, saffron, cream and oyster or clam juice. Stir and add the slaked cornflour and cook until thickened. Remove from heat and whisk in the walnut oil under a steady stream. Add vinegar and season to taste.

Slice the scallops fairly thinly. Cut potatoes into very thin slices with a mandolin cutter and marinate in about a tablespoon of olive oil with chopped thyme. Butter an ovenproof plate and arrange scallop slices on it. Cook for five minutes in the oven at 150°C/300°F/Gas 3. Cook the potatoes on a griddle pan on both sides until soft.

Arrange scallop medallions and potato slices in a circle on each plate. Dress aromatic salad with olive oil, balsamic vinegar, salt and pepper. Place salad in centre of each plate. Spoon saffron vinaigrette over potatoes and scallops. Slice artichoke very thinly with a mandolin cutter and deep-fry until crisp.

Garnish each plate with the dressing, slivers of truffle, balsamic vinegar and fried artichoke slices.

QE2

# Rillet of Salmon with Crayfish and Cucumber

### Serves 6

*450g (1lb) fresh salmon, poached*
*80g (3oz) softened butter*
*4 tablespoons mayonnaise*
*salt and freshly ground pepper*
*½ bunch chives, chopped*
*juice of ½ lime*
*6 slices smoked salmon, diced*

## Cucumber Salad

*1 cucumber*
*3 tablespoons vegetable oil*
*2 tablespoons white wine vinegar*
*1 teaspoon sugar*
*fresh dill, chopped*
*salt and freshly ground pepper*

## Garnish

*lettuce leaves in season*
*strips of red or green peppers*
*chopped spring onions or dill sprigs*
*18 poached crayfish*

To make the rillets, flake the poached salmon and chill. Cream the butter and whisk in the mayonnaise. Add the flaked salmon, season with salt and pepper and beat until smooth. Transfer to a bowl and add the chives, lime juice and the smoked salmon. Adjust seasoning if necessary.

To make the cucumber salad, peel the cucumber, cut in half lengthways and scrape out the seeds. Slice the cucumber and marinade in the dressing, made by whisking together the remaining ingredients.

Arrange the salmon mixture in a ring on each plate, garnish with salad leaves and the cucumber salad and decorate with strips of red or green peppers, spring onion (or dill) and crayfish.

# Shellfish Terrine

### Serves 8

*2 bay leaves*
*1 bunch thyme*
*1 bunch parsley*
*1 carrot, diced*
*1 onion, diced*
*1 fennel bulb, diced*
*1 leek, diced*
*2 garlic cloves, crushed*
*3 tablespoons olive oil*
*250ml (9fl oz) white wine*
*salt and white pepper*
*20 strands saffron*
*1 litre (1¾ pints) fish stock*
*2 lobster tails*
*5 jumbo prawns*
*5 large scallops, white part only*
*400g (14oz) salmon fillets*
*300g (11oz) spinach leaves*
*15 leaves gelatine, soaked in a little cold*
*water*
*1 carrot cut into thin strips with a*
*potato peeler*
*10 stuffed green Spanish olives*

## To Clarify the Fish Stock:
*300g (11oz) white fish*
*4 egg whites*

Combine bay leaves, thyme and parsley into a bouquet garni.

Sauté the diced vegetables and the garlic in one tablespoon olive oil. Add the white wine, salt and pepper and half the saffron strands. Leave to reduce for a couple of minutes, then add the fish stock and cook for twenty minutes and strain.

Poach the shellfish – lobster tails, jumbo prawns and scallops – in the liquid and set aside. Cut the salmon into long strips – just a bit

SHELLFISH TERRINE

heat and wait a little for the residue to settle, then strain through a cloth or very fine sieve.

Stir squeezed gelatine into the fish stock. Steam the carrot strips for about five minutes. Line a terrine with clingfilm and carrot strips, then pour in about half a centimetre of the fish stock. Let it set a little, then add some of the fish and shellfish and cover with more fish stock. Let it set and repeat the operation, placing stuffed olives between the fish and the shellfish. Fill up terrine in this way and cover top with carrot strips. Refrigerate for five hours and serve cut into slices.

shorter than then length of the terrine – and sear them in the remaining two tablespoons of olive oil. Blanch the spinach for less than a minute and refresh in cold water. Pat dry with kitchen paper. Wrap the fish and shellfish completely with the spinach leaves.

To clarify the fish stock, mince the white fish and mix with the egg white and cooled fish stock. Add remaining saffron and bring back to a slow simmer. Simmer for five minutes, remove from

# Braised Oxtail Salad with Tomato Chutney

**Serves 4**

900–1,100g (2–2½ lb) oxtail
    cut into 5cm (2in) pieces
2 tablespoons sea salt
freshly ground black pepper
4 tablespoons vegetable oil
2 cups mirepoix (diced carrots, celery,
    onions and leek)
2 tablespoons tomato paste
¼ cup balsamic vinegar
¼ cup port
1 cup red wine
1 bouquet garni

## Marinade

2 shallots, chopped
2 cloves garlic, chopped
4 tablespoons chopped parsley
2 tablespoons Dijon mustard
3 tablespoons red wine vinegar
1 cup olive oil
salt and freshly ground black pepper

## Chutney

5 ripe tomatoes
1 tablespoon brown sugar
3 tablespoons red wine vinegar
1 small chilli
½ teaspoon crushed garlic
2 tablespoons chopped ginger
salt and pepper

## Garnish

225g (½lb) mixed salad (baby spinach, radicchio,
    curly endive)
2 tablespoons chopped fresh herbs
    (chervil, tarragon, basil, flat-leaf parsley)
4 tablespoons vinaigrette dressing

Season the oxtail with salt and freshly ground black pepper, then sear in vegetable oil over medium-high heat until well-browned. Remove oxtail and keep warm. Reduce heat and add mirepoix and tomato paste and stir. Fry lightly for a few minutes, drain off excess fat. Deglaze with balsamic vinegar, port and red wine. Reduce until all the liquid has evaporated, return oxtail to saucepan and add just enough water to cover meat and vegetables. Bring to boil and simmer until the oxtail is tender which can take up to three hours. Take the oxtail out of the liquid and when cool enough to handle, strip all the meat from the bones and cut into 2½cm (1in) strips. Strain the stock and set to cool and when quite cold, remove all grease. Combine all the ingredients for the marinade together. Marinate the meat in the mixture and add four tablespoons of the degreased, strained oxtail stock.

To make the chutney, peel, seed and dice the tomatoes. Caramelize the sugar and add the red wine vinegar. Bring to boil and add the remaining ingredients. Lower heat and simmer for fifteen minutes. If necessary, sprinkle a spoonful of water into the mixture. Refrigerate until used.

Divide salad between four plates, sprinkle with chopped herbs and vinaigrette. Lift oxtail out of the marinade and place on top of the salad with a tablespoon of the chutney.

# Marinated Beef Fillet with Herbs

## Serves 4

*400g (14oz) beef fillet (tenderloin)*
*100g (3½oz) spinach*
*15 basil leaves*
*1 clove garlic, crushed*
*1 tablespoon almonds*
*4 tablespoons olive oil*
*2 handfuls mixed seasonal lettuce*
*4 tablespoons vinaigrette for the lettuce*
*little extra olive oil for dressing*
*salt and freshly ground black pepper*

Cut the beef fillet in half lengthways – but do not cut right through – so that you have one large piece. Put the meat on top of a large sheet of clingfilm on a board and press it out with your hands as thinly as possible.

Wash, drain and thoroughly dry the spinach. Put into a food processor together with the basil, crushed garlic and almonds and process, adding the olive oil gradually. Spread this mixture over the meat and roll up. Wrap the meat roll in clingfilm and put into the freezer for four to five hours.

Take the beef roulade out of the freezer half an hour before serving. Divide lettuce leaves between four plates and sprinkle with vinaigrette dressing. Cut the beef roulade into very thin slices with a sharp kitchen knife and lay the slices around the salad. Sprinkle with a little olive oil and season with salt and freshly ground black pepper.

Serve with fresh walnut bread.

# Vinaigrette

## Serves 4

*2 shallots, finely diced*
*salt, pepper, pinch of icing sugar*
*100ml (3½fl oz) consommé*
*(or fish fond according to use)*
*2 tablespoons sherry or lemon vinegar*
*2 tablespoon sherry*
*4 tablespoons walnut oil*
*4 tablespoons grape seed oil*
*½ tablespoon Dijon mustard*

Blanch the diced shallots for thirty seconds. Refresh with cold water. Dissolve salt, pepper and sugar in consommé or fish fond. Mix together consommé, vinegar and sherry. Add shallots and whisk together with the oils and mustard.

For herb vinaigrette add two tablespoons of chopped herbs such as chives, parsley, tarragon and chervil.

QE2

# Goose-liver Medallions with Poached Peaches

### Serves 4

*400ml (14fl oz) veal stock*
*50g (2oz) brown sugar*
*200ml (7fl oz) peach eau-de-vie*
*1 stick cinnamon*
*4 fresh peaches, skinned and halved*
*4 fresh goose-liver medallions 1cm (½ in) thick*
*2 shallots, chopped*
*100ml (3½ fl oz) raspberry vinegar*
*salt and white pepper*

Heat the veal stock and reduce to half. Dissolve the brown sugar in a little water, add a third of the peach eau-de-vie and the cinnamon stick. Heat slowly and poach the skinned and halved peaches in the syrup. Heat a non-stick frying pan and sear the goose-liver medallions for a few seconds on each side. Remove and keep warm. Sauté the chopped shallots in the fat released from the goose-liver, add the raspberry vinegar and flambé with the remaining peach eau-de-vie. Add the reduced veal stock, cook for one minute, then add the seared goose-liver. Season.

Serve garnished with the peach halves lifted from the syrup with a slotted spoon.

GOOSE-LIVER MEDALLIONS
WITH POACHED PEACHES

48

# Sorbets

On the QE2 sorbets are of course prepared in an ice-cream maker. If this is not available, freeze in an ordinary freezer breaking up the mixture every thirty minutes – the more you stir, the lighter the sorbet will be. Egg whites are lightly beaten and stirred into the mixture before it is put into the ice-cream maker, but if using a freezer, whisk the egg whites until stiff and fold into the half-frozen mixture.

The QE2 kitchens use pasteurized egg whites for their sorbets, but if you are worried about including uncooked egg, this can be left out. The resulting sorbet will be just a little less airy.

SORBETS

QE2

(FROM TOP, CLOCKWISE)
PINEAPPLE SORBET; ORANGE CAMPARI SORBET;
KIWI SORBET; PEACH SORBET; APPLE GINGER
SORBET; LEMON SORBET

SORBETS

QE2

## · Sorbets ·

Simple Sugar Syrup
Lime Sorbet
Pineapple Sorbet
Orange Campari Sorbet
Raspberry Sorbet
Lemon Sorbet
Peach or Kiwi Sorbet
Gin Fizz Sorbet
Lemon and Vodka Sorbet
Apple Ginger Sorbet

# Simple Sugar Syrup

For sorbets, cold soups, etc.

*500g (18oz) caster sugar*
*500ml (18fl oz) water*

Dissolve sugar in water, bring to boil and simmer for fifteen minutes. Leave to cool and store in a cold place.

# Lime Sorbet

About 10 scoops

*350g (12oz) caster sugar*
*500ml (18fl oz) water*
*juice and zest of 10 limes*

Dissolve sugar in water, bring to the boil and simmer for fifteen minutes. Add the lime zest to the sugar syrup and leave to infuse. When the syrup has cooled down, add the lime juice and strain through a fine sieve. Freeze as described on page 49.

# Pineapple Sorbet

About 20 scoops

*200g (7oz) caster sugar*
*300ml (11fl oz) water*
*1 litre (1¼ pints) unsweetened pineapple juice*
*1 egg white*

Dissolve sugar in water, bring to the boil and simmer for fifteen minutes. Add pineapple juice and allow to cool. Whisk egg white lightly, add to cooled juice then freeze as described on page 49.

# Orange Campari Sorbet

**About 20 scoops**

*100g (3½ oz) caster sugar*
*500ml (18fl oz) water*
*500ml (18fl oz) unsweetened orange juice*
*200ml (7fl oz) Campari*
*1 egg white*

Dissolve sugar in water, bring to the boil and simmer for fifteen minutes. Remove from heat and allow to cool. Add orange juice and Campari. Lightly beat egg white and add then freeze as described on page 49.

# Lemon Sorbet

**About 20 scoops**

*230g (8oz) caster sugar*
*600ml (21½ fl oz) water*
*1 teaspoon grated lemon rind*
*180ml (6½ fl oz) lemon juice*
*1 egg white*

Dissolve sugar in water, bring to the boil, add lemon rind and simmer for fifteen minutes. Allow to cool, strain and add lemon juice. Add lightly beaten egg white then freeze as described on page 49.

# Raspberry Sorbet

**About 20 scoops**

*320g (12oz) caster sugar*
*400ml (14fl oz) water*
*300g (11oz) unsweetened raspberry purée*
*2 tablespoons lemon juice*
*2 tablespoons raspberry eau-de-vie or Kirsch*
*1 egg white*

Dissolve sugar in water, bring to the boil and simmer for fifteen minutes. Remove from heat, add fruit purée, lemon juice and eau-de-vie or Kirsch and allow to cool. Add lightly whisked egg white and freeze as described on page 49.

# Peach or Kiwi Sorbet

**About 20 scoops**

*300g (11oz) caster sugar*
*500ml (18fl oz) water*
*1kg (2¼ lb) peach or kiwi puree*
*1 egg white*

Dissolve sugar in water, bring to the boil and simmer for fifteen minutes. Allow to cool, add fruit purée and lightly beaten egg white and freeze as described on page 49.

QE2

# Gin Fizz Sorbet

**Serves 8**

*2 cups simple sugar syrup (see page 50)*
*6 tablespoons gin*
*6 tablespoons Campari*
*juice 1 lemon*
*1 cup soda water*
*2 egg whites*

Combine all the ingredients except the egg whites. Lightly beat the egg whites add to other ingredients then freeze as described on page 49.

# Lemon and Vodka Sorbet

**About 10 scoops**

*300g (11oz) caster sugar*
*500ml (18fl oz) water*
*3 tablespoons lemon juice*
*5 tablespoons vodka*
*½ egg white*

Dissolve sugar in water, bring to the boil and simmer for fifteen minutes. Remove from heat add lemon juice and vodka and allow to cool. Whisk egg white lightly, add and then freeze as described on page 49.

## QE2
### TIPS · FROM · THE · CHEFS

Make sure that all fruit is blended to a smooth purée then sieve fruit such as blackberries, raspberries and red currants to get rid of the pips.

Allow the mixture to become ice-cold before putting it into the ice-cream maker or freezing in trays.

The finished sorbet can be piped or spooned into any fancy glass or into the shells of fresh fruits such as oranges, lemons, peaches, etc. To prepare the fruit, cut a lid off the top, carefully remove the flesh of the fruit which can be used in the sorbet, and deep-freeze the shell. Use a piping bag or spoon to fill the shells with the sorbet then replace the lids. All this can be done in advance.

# Apple Ginger Sorbet

**About 20 scoops**

*125g (4½oz) caster sugar*
*1 litre (1¾ pints) unsweetened apple juice*
*1 tablespoon fresh ginger, finely chopped*
*120ml (4½fl oz) Calvados*
*1 egg white*

Dissolve sugar in apple juice, heat slowly and add ginger. Remove from heat, add Calvados and allow to cool. Allow to infuse for two hours. Strain, add lightly whipped egg white and then freeze as described on page 49.

# Fruits of the Sea

*QE2 passengers are very partial to lobster – 37,966 Maine lobsters were consumed during 1998, 624 on a transatlantic crossing alone. These come on board live and are prepared for the table, as required, daily – a favourite way being just steamed or grilled with melted butter and fresh herbs, though QE2 chefs take great pride in the more elaborate presentations such as Lobster Thermidor and Lobster a l'Americaine. Lobster QE2 is a rather spectacular way of using lobster tails – 3,416 lb were used in 1998 – the lobster meat is wrapped in spinach leaves and puff pastry and baked, served with delicate beurre blanc flecked with chives.*

*One might think that fresh fish could be purchased in any harbour town in the world, but this does not always work out. Even when ordered well in advance, it is possible to find on arrival that no fresh fish can be delivered. A small restaurant may be able to have its orders filled, but the huge needs of the QE2 are another matter. On the other hand, visits to local markets often make for splendid combinations in dishes where a variety of fish is used – particularly Fisherman's Pot, a great favourite in the Wardroom where the same dishes are on the menu as in the QE2 restaurants. Red Mullet should really go into Fisherman's Pot, but on one occasion when the local fish market could not supply the required quantity and the beautifully fresh fish was too good to miss, some were bought and used for an on board cookery demonstration!*

## · Fish ·

Steamed Turbot with Lobster Mousse

Salmon Steaks en Papillote

Glazed Red Mullet

Lobster QE2

Fillet of Red Snapper al Brodetto

Sesame Crusted Tuna Steak
in Wasabi Sauce

QE2 Fisherman's Pot

Salmon Fillet with Onion Risotto

Saltimbocca of Turbot with Linguini

Pavé of Turbot
on a Bed of seared Vermont Apples

Grilled Sea Bass with Braised Leeks
and Thyme

# Steamed Turbot with Lobster Mousse

### Serves 4

*225g (8oz) cooked lobster meat*
*2 tablespoons melted butter*
*2 egg yolks*
*½ cup double cream*
*salt and pepper*
*2 egg whites*
*4 thick turbot slices, weighing about 140–170g*
*(5–6oz) each*
*1 cup dry white wine*
*½ cup fish stock*
*juice and grated rind of 1 lemon*
*3 tablespoons butter*

Purée the lobster meat in a food processor or blender. Mix together melted butter, egg yolks and half the cream. Fold in the puréed lobster meat and season with salt and pepper. Whisk egg whites until stiff and fold into the mixture.

Preheat the oven to 180°C / 350°F / Gas 4. Butter a shallow flame- and ovenproof dish. Place turbot in the dish in a single layer and sprinkle with salt and pepper. Add white wine, fish stock, lemon juice and the grated lemon rind. Spread the lobster mousse thickly over the fish slices. Place dish over direct heat to bring liquid to boil, then transfer the dish to the oven for twenty to twenty five minutes. Remove fish from the baking dish and keep warm. Add remaining cream to the liquid in the dish and simmer briefly to reduce. Remove from heat and whisk in the butter in small flakes.

Serve sauce with the fish.

FRUITS OF THE SEA

QE2

# Salmon Steaks en Papillote

Serves 4

*4 salmon steaks, weighing about 200g (7oz) each*
*salt and pepper*
*½ cup dry white wine*
*3 shallots, finely chopped*
*½ cup finely chopped walnuts*
*2 hard-boiled eggs, chopped*
*1 tablespoon finely chopped dill*
*4 thin lemon slices*

Preheat the oven to 190°C / 375°F / Gas 5. Butter four 20cm (8in) squares of aluminium foil. Set one salmon steak in the centre of each square. Sprinkle with salt and pepper, the white wine and the chopped ingredients. Top each steak with a lemon slice. Fold the squares to make four airtight packages. Place parcels on a baking sheet and bake for ten minutes.

Serve in the foil packages, slit open.

# Glazed Red Mullet

Serves 4

*2 red mullet*
*2 tablespoons honey*
*50ml (2fl oz) olive oil*
*salt*
*2 tablespoons chopped basil*
*2 tomatoes*
*pesto and strips of deep-fried aubergine skin*
*      to garnish*

Clean and fillet the fish. Combine honey, olive oil and a pinch of salt. Brush over red mullet fillets and grill.

Arrange fillets on plates, garnish with basil, blanched tomato segments and pesto. Top with deep-fried aubergine skins.

## QE2

TRANSATLANTIC • CROSSING

*The first Transatlantic crossing on the QE2 in 1969 took four days, sixteen hours and thirty-six minutes (shortened on a later crossing to 102 hours) and that allowed for a stop at Le Havre before heading West. In recent years the crossing has been extended, first, to five, and finally, to six days, taking a more Southern route to avoid bad weather – a move obviously approved by passengers, for bookings increased considerably. 'It is wonderful' said an American business man. 'I fly to Europe and after some strenuous meetings I take the leisurely route back to relax . No strain. No stress. No jet lag – you get an extra hour's sleep each night. I wish it'd take longer still so that I could enjoy all the amenities. And have some more of that superb food.' The same applies to holiday makers on both sides of the Atlantic – fly one way and have an extra holiday on the QE2 – in fact over 25,000 made that choice last year. For real luxury there's of course British Airways Sleeper Service, which is practically a miniature holiday on its own. Between May and September there are usually eleven Transatlantic round trips when the ship literally 'turns round' in either New York or Southampton for the return journey and some passengers never get off the ship at all – simply enjoying a twelve-day holiday on board.*

# Lobster QE2

**Serves 4**

*4 lobster tails*
*300g (11oz) salmon fillet*
*200ml (7fl oz) double cream*
*salt and pepper*
*200g (7oz) spinach leaves*
*black truffle*
*800g (29oz) puff pastry*
*2 egg yolks*

## Butter Sauce

*250g (9oz) butter*
*½ tablespoon butter*
*2 shallots, finely chopped*
*30g (I generous oz) ginger, finely chopped*
*1 cup dry white wine*
*1 tablespoon lemon juice or white wine vinegar*
*salt and pepper*
*1 tablespoon chopped chives*

Blanch the lobster tails for two minutes. Remove shell but leave the tips attached to the flesh.

Skin and bone salmon fillet, and cut into small pieces. Chill salmon and cream before processing. Add seasoning whilst processing.

Blanch the spinach leaves very quickly and refresh with cold water. Drain, express all moisture and dry on kitchen paper. Cut open the lobster tails and remove dark ligament. Slice the truffle very thinly and place the slices down the centre of the opened lobster tails. Top with salmon mousse and wrap with spinach. Roll out the puff pastry and cut into four pieces to enclose the lobster tails. Wrap each lobster tail with the puff pastry and brush with egg yolks lightly beaten with a little water. Bake at 200°C / 400°F / Gas 6 for seventeen minutes.

Meanwhile prepare the butter sauce. Cut the 250g (9oz) of butter into 1cm (½ in) cubes. Melt the half tablespoon of butter and gently sweat the shallots and ginger. Add white wine and lemon juice (or white wine vinegar) and reduce until only a quarter of the liquid is left, then strain. Add the diced butter gradually, whisking continuously until you have a silky, smooth sauce, do not allow the mixture to boil. Add seasoning and keep warm, adding chopped chives just before serving.

Slice the lobster tails, but leave enough for the end to stand up. Arrange on plates and surround with the sauce.

QE2

# Fillet of Red Snapper al Brodetto

**Serves 4**

*4 tablespoons olive oil*
*4 red snapper fillets, weighing about 160g*
        *(5–6oz) each*
*1 clove garlic, very finely chopped*
*4 Little Neck clams*
*8 mussels*
*125ml (4fl oz) white wine*
*450g (1lb) ripe tomatoes, peeled and coarsely*
        *chopped*
*4 fresh basil leaves*
*1 teaspoon chopped flat-leaf parsley*
*¼ teaspoon oregano*
*salt and freshly ground black pepper*

Heat the oil in a large, heavy frying pan over medium heat and sear the fillets for about two minutes on each side, turning them carefully using a spatula. Remove from pan and keep warm. Put the garlic, clams and mussels in the same frying pan and sweat for a few minutes. Add white wine, tomatoes, basil, parsley, oregano and season with salt and pepper. Cover pan and cook for ten minutes. Put the fillets back into the frying pan to finish cooking.

Remove cooked fish from the sauce, scrape off any adhering sauce and set the fish under a hot grill to crisp. Arrange mussels, clams and sauce on a big platter, put fillets on top and serve.

FRUITS OF THE SEA

QE2

# Sesame Crusted Tuna Steak in Wasabi Sauce

**Serves 6**

*1 bottle (375ml / 13½ fl oz) balsamic vinegar*
*6 tuna steaks, weighing about 170g (6oz) each*
*2 tablespoons oyster sauce*
*½ cup sesame seeds, roasted*
*salt and pepper*
*2 large carrots, cut into long strips*
*1 leek, cut into long strips*

## Wasabi Sauce

*1 cup mayonnaise*
*1 tablespoon Worcestershire sauce*
*1 tablespoon English mustard*
*1 tablespoon fish sauce*
*⅓ cup chicken broth*
*2 tablespoons lemon juice*
*½ tablespoon soy sauce*
*⅓ tablespoon Wasabi powder*

To make the Wasabi Sauce mix together mayonnaise, Worcestershire sauce, fish sauce, chicken broth, lemon juice, soy sauce and Wasabi powder.

Reduce the balsamic vinegar over medium heat until thickened. Cool and pour into a small jug or squeeze bottle. Brush the tuna steaks with oyster sauce and cover sides with sesame seeds. Season to taste and grill the steaks to rare. Blanch the carrots and leeks in salted water and arrange in the centre of the plate. Place the steaks on top. Circle the balsamic vinegar over the fish, then streak the Wasabi sauce over the top.

SESAME CRUSTED TUNA STEAK
IN WASABI SAUCE (LEFT)

# QE2 Fisherman's Pot

Serves 4

*½ lb (225g) rock fish*
*½ lb (225g) monkfish*
*4 crayfish*
*4 small red mullet*
*16 mussels*
*4 large scallops*
*16 Manila clams/vongole*
*1 large onion*
*1 fennel bulb*
*1 carrot*
*1 leek*
*2 cloves garlic*
*2 tomatoes*
*2 tablespoons olive oil*
*2 bay leaves*
*20 strands saffron*
*¼ cup Pernod*
*1 cup dry white wine*
*1¼ litres (2 pints) fish stock*
*salt and pepper*

Clean, cut and rinse all the fish and shellfish in salted water. The red mullet should be left whole. Dice the onion, fennel, carrot and leek and finely chop the garlic. Peel and roughly chop the tomatoes. Heat two tablespoons of olive oil in a saucepan and sauté the vegetables and garlic until tender. Add the chopped tomatoes, bay leaves and saffron strands and deglaze with the Pernod. Add white wine and fish stock and cook for fifteen minutes at slow boil. Gently lay the fish and shellfish into the pan and cover. Simmer slowly for ten minutes. Season and remove the fish from the pan.

Divide fish between four bowls, then pour the broth over the fish and serve with French bread and the rouille.

# Rouille

*3 large garlic cloves*
*½ teaspoon salt*
*2 egg yolks*
*1 cup extra-virgin olive oil*
*pinch saffron powder*
*½ teaspoon cayenne pepper*

For the rouille, pound the garlic with the salt until it resembles a paste. Add the egg yolks. Whisk in the extra-virgin olive oil slowly, drop by drop, as for mayonnaise. Add the saffron and cayenne pepper.

MANILA CLAMS (LEFT)
QE2 FISHERMAN'S POT (RIGHT)

FRUITS OF THE SEA

QE2

QE2

# Salmon Fillet with Onion Risotto

**Serves 4**

*4 salmon escallops,*
        *each weighing about 140–160g (4½–5oz)*
*salt and freshly ground pepper*
*juice ½ lemon*
*butter*

## Onion Risotto

*2 tablespoons butter*
*1 red onion, cut into big wedges*
*½ clove garlic, crushed*
*1 cup Arborio rice*
*3 cups vegetable bouillon*
*salt and freshly ground black pepper*
*½ cup double cream*

## Sauce

*1 bottle red wine*
*½ cup port*
*2 shallots, diced*
*½ bay leaf*
*2 tablespoons butter cut into small dice*

## Garnish

*12 green asparagus spears*
*butter for frying*

For the risotto, melt butter in a thick saucepan. Add onion and garlic and sweat until translucent. Put the rice in a sieve and rinse under running tap until water runs clear. Shake dry. Add rice to the onion and stir gently until rice is hand-warm and translucent. Add hot vegetable bouillon little by little – the rice should have absorbed the liquid before any more is added. Cook until *al dente*. Season to taste. Add cream just before serving.

Season the salmon escallops with salt, freshly ground pepper and lemon juice. Melt butter in a non-stick frying pan and seal escallops on both sides, then grill for three minutes on each side. Cover with aluminium foil and keep warm.

To prepare the sauce use a small saucepan and pour in red wine and port. Add shallots and bay leaf and reduce over high heat to one third. Strain and whisk in the butter – the sauce should have a very light consistency. To prepare garnish cut off asparagus stems and gently pan-fry the uncooked spears in butter until tender.

Divide risotto between four plates, place fish on top and surround with the sauce. Garnish with the fried asparagus spears.

QE2

Kennels on the QE2 are in keeping with the requirements of pampered pets – with a kennel maid in attendance, room for walkies and even a London lamp post for 'convenience'. Fifty pounds of dog biscuits are carried on each Transatlantic trip as well as the requisite amount of pet food, 'but if a pet is used to a special diet, we provide it' says Karl Winkler. No doubt after due consideration of the menu and Chef's suggestions...

At present kennel space is usually available, but wait until word gets round the canine world when the quarantine laws are lifted – booking could be as difficult as getting into an exclusive restaurant.

QE2

# Saltimbocca of Turbot with Linguini

*Serves 4*

8 turbot escallops weighing 60–80g
    *(2–3oz) each*
*salt and white pepper*
*a little freshly squeezed lemon juice*
*8 slices pancetta*
*8 sage leaves*
*¼ cup clarified butter for frying*
*¼ cup Marsala*
*¼ cup fish stock*
*1 cup veal stock*

## To Serve:

*450g (1lb ) linguini*
*1 cup tomato sauce (see page 108)*
*¼ cup basil infused olive oil*
*sage leaves fried in batter*

SALTIMBOCCA OF TURBOT
WITH LINGUINI

Flatten the fish escallops lightly and season with salt, white pepper and lemon juice. Put a slice of pancetta and a sage leaf on top of each escallop and press down firmly. Heat clarified butter in a frying pan and fry fish on both sides, taking care that the pancetta and sage leaf stay firmly attached (you can fasten them with a wooden toothpick, but it should not be necessary). Keep the escallops hot. Pour the Marsala into a saucepan and reduce over medium heat to half. Add the fish stock and the veal stock and continue reducing to half.

Cook the linguini in boiling salted water until *al dente*, drain and divide between four plates. Put two escallops on top of each linguini portion. Add heated tomato sauce to Marsala sauce and blend. Swirl in basil-infused olive oil. Pour over fish and pasta and decorate with sage leaves fried in batter.

F R U I T S   O F   T H E   S E A

QE2

## QE2

VIEW · FROM · THE · GALLEY

*Last year 32,366 lbs of fresh asparagus were consumed on the QE2, 6,917 lbs of Dover sole and 3,700 1-oz jars of Beluga caviar. The cellars are stocked with thirty-seven different wines from eleven countries and four continents and there is a selection of twenty-one types of cigars, but the most expensive item – two-and-a half times the value of Beluga caviar –is saffron: one-and-a-half packets are used daily, 547½ packets annually.*

# Pavé of Turbot on a Bed of seared Vermont Apples

**Serves 4**

8 turbot fillets
3 teaspoons curry powder
1 teaspoon cumin
100ml (3½ fl oz) extra-virgin olive oil
salt and pepper
2 red Vermont apples, sliced
brown sugar
sprigs of dill to garnish

## Sauce

100ml (3½fl oz) olive oil
1 onion, sliced
4 cloves garlic
4 tablespoons curry powder
25g (1oz) cumin
1 heaped tablespoon chopped ginger
3 cloves
thyme
1 star anise
1 bay leaf
1 teaspoon tomato paste
500ml (18fl oz) chicken stock
200ml (7fl oz) coconut milk
3 red Vermont apples, diced

Rub the fish on one side only with curry powder, cumin, a little extra-virgin olive oil, salt and pepper. Steam the fish. Rub the sliced apples with oil, dust with brown sugar and sear in a griddle pan.

To make the sauce, put the olive oil in a very hot pan and cook the onion and garlic for five minutes, then add the curry powder, cumin, ginger, cloves, thyme, star anise and bay leaf. Cook gently for ten minutes, add tomato paste, chicken stock and coconut milk and cook for twenty minutes. Remove bay leaf, cloves and star anise. Add the diced apples.

Arrange the seared apple slices on plates, top with two slices of turbot per plate, surround with sauce and garnish with sprigs of dill.

PAVÉ OF TURBOT ON A BED OF
SEARED VERMONT APPLES

# Grilled Sea Bass with Braised Leeks and Thyme

**Serves 4**

*4 sea bass fillets, weighing 225g (8oz) each*
*juice of 1 lemon*
*2 leeks, diced into 5cm (2 inch) batons*
*1 tablespoon butter*
*5 tablespoons white wine*
*1 cup double cream*
*salt and pepper*

## Fish and Thyme Jus

*450g (1lb) fish bones, rinsed*
*½ cup olive oil*
*1 onion, diced*
*½ cup dry white wine*
*sprig thyme*
*1 cup veal stock*

## Garnish

*sautéed oyster mushrooms*
*small new potatoes*
*strips of leek, blanched, patted dry and crisped in*
*the oven on waxed paper at lowest setting*

For the sauce, sauté the fish bones in olive oil until lightly browned. Add the onion and stir over low heat until onion is transparent. Pour in the white wine and reduce to half. Add thyme and veal stock and reduce to half. Simmer until thickened. Strain and keep warm.

Season fish fillets with salt, pepper and lemon juice.

Sauté leek batons in butter until translucent. Add white wine and reduce until liquid has evaporated. Pour in the double cream and simmer until leeks are cooked and the cream reduced. Season to taste. Grill the fish on both sides – do not overcook

Arrange leeks in the centre of plates and place fish on top. Pour the sauce around the dish and garnish with oyster mushrooms, new potatoes and crisped leek strips.

## QE2

### W O R L D · C R U I S E S

There have been twenty-four World Cruises to date – the first in 1975. For some passengers it is a 'once in a lifetime' experience, carefully saved for over the years – others come every year, thus forming one of the most exclusive clubs in the world. The same dish will not appear twice on the menu – not even during a World Cruise lasting 100 days. Passengers have their definite favourites, often calling for a dish they enjoyed many years back and then the recipe will have to be found in the archives – or re-created from Chef's memory. Calorie counts and other nutritional values are always listed against the dishes on the Spa menu. Except on World Cruises in the Queen's Grill: one faithful 'World Cruiser' – he rejoins the ship every year, occupying two penthouses as well as two staterooms – will not have his enjoyment marred by facts and at his request calorie counts and other nutritional values are omitted from the Queen's Grill menus. Any passenger wishing to know these will have to make discreet enquiries via the Mâitre d'!

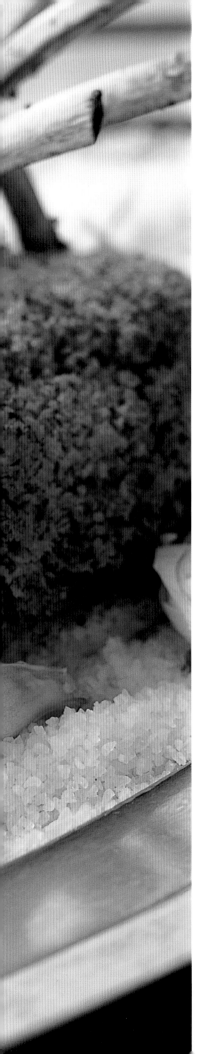

# Meat, Poultry and Game

*A*bout three million meals a year are served on the QE2 – in 1998 14,034 lbs of beef sirloin were used, 36,631 lbs of veal bones for jus alone – and on a transatlantic crossing 800 to 900 portions of Beef Wellington are prepared: the truly amazing fact is that they are prepared to perfection each and every time. Order your Beef Wellington medium-rare and that is exactly how it will be served. Commendable in a small restaurant, but consider the vast scale of operation.

Nor are all dishes haute cuisine – the further from home, the greater the talk about home cooking and that is when country dishes such as Beef Pot Roast and BBQ Braised Short Ribs are on the menu. In foreign ports, travellers can enjoy native cuisine and experiencing the difference between how a dish is made in its homeland and how it translates to Western tables can enhance an appreciation for one or the other – or both.

Quite a number of passengers have been on board fifty or sixty times – including the woman who had a separate stateroom booked for her teddy bears (one always chosen to keep her company at dinner) – and they have established their favourite dishes after lengthy deliberations. Others pick a winner straight away: Patrick Moore, one of the star lecturers on the QE2 loved the Chicken Tikka Masala and the Chicken Korma prepared by the Indian Chefs at 'first taste'.

The QE2 has always been famous for its roasts – prime-quality meat cooked to perfection. On the bone, as it should be.

ROAST HERBED RACKS OF LAMB WITH GARLIC SAUCE

## · Meat, Poultry and Game ·

# Braised Lamb Shanks with Bean Stew

### Serves 4

2½kg (4lb) lamb hind shanks, trimmed
½ cup olive oil
salt and crushed peppercorns
2 onions, diced
2 cloves garlic, crushed
1 carrot, cut into big cubes
1 stick of celery, diced
1 turnip, cut into big cubes
1 tablespoon tomato paste
1 cup red wine
2 cups chicken stock
½ cup Borlotti beans, soaked overnight in water
½ cup white dried haricot beans, soaked overnight
    in water
2 bay leaves
1 sprig rosemary
1 sprig thyme
5 cups tinned tomatoes, cut into chunks
3 tablespoons chopped fresh herbs
    (basil, tarragon, parsley)

Sear the shanks in hot olive oil in a casserole and season with salt and crushed peppercorns. Remove and keep warm. Sweat onions and garlic in the same oil until translucent. Add carrot, celery and turnip. Fry lightly for a few minutes. Add tomato paste, stir to incorporate, then pour in the red wine and reduce to half. Pour in the chicken stock, add soaked and drained beans, bay leaves, rosemary and thyme. Place lamb shanks in casserole and simmer for eighty to ninety minutes, until shanks are almost done, then add tomatoes and simmer for another thirty minutes. Serve sprinkled with chopped herbs.

MEAT, POULTRY AND GAME

QE2

QE2

# Roast Herbed Racks of Lamb with Garlic Sauce

Serves 6

*½ cup dry breadcrumbs*
*¼ teaspoon dried chilli*
*6 cloves garlic, crushed*
*1 tablespoon chopped rosemary*
*¼ cup chopped parsley*
*50g (2oz) melted butter*
*salt*
*3 tablespoons olive oil*
*2 tablespoons Dijon mustard*
*2 racks of lamb, weighing 1,350g (3lb) in total*

## Garlic Sauce

*450g (1lb) lean lamb trimmings*
*2 tablespoons vegetable oil*
*120g (4oz) onions, chopped*
*60g (2oz) celery, coarsely chopped*
*120g (4oz) carrots, coarsely chopped*
*2 tablespoons tomato paste*
*½ cup red wine*
*sprig of rosemary*
*sprig of thyme*
*10 black peppercorns, crushed*
*1 bay leaf*
*6 cloves garlic, peeled*
*1⅛ litre (2 pints) veal stock*
*salt*

To make the sauce sear the lamb trimmings in oil, then add onions, celery and carrots and brown lightly. Add tomato paste and red wine. Reduce until almost evaporated. Add rosemary, thyme, crushed peppercorns, bay leaf and garlic, stir and add the veal stock. Simmer for one hour over low heat, skimming off any fat and impurities that rise to the surface. Strain, adjust seasoning if necessary and reduce to 1½ cups. Keep warm.

Combine breadcrumbs, chilli, garlic, rosemary, parsley, melted butter and seasoning. Season the racks with salt and rub with olive oil, then place on roasting racks and roast for ten minutes at 180°C / 350°F / Gas 4. Spread mustard and a thin layer of the herb mixture over the meat and roast for another ten minutes at the same temperature. Remove from oven and keep in a warm place for at least ten minutes before carving.

QE2

# Rack of Lamb with Dijon Mustard Crust

Serves 4

2 tablespoons olive oil
2 racks of lamb, weighing about 1¼ kg (3lb) in
      total
salt and black pepper

## Dijon Mustard Crust

2 tablespoons chopped shallots
2 tablespoons chopped garlic
4 tablespoons olive oil
²⁄₃ cup fresh white breadcrumbs
1 sprig rosemary, chopped
2 tablespoons chopped parsley
salt and freshly ground black pepper
¼ cup Dijon mustard

## Vegetables for roasting

1 medium-sized onion, chopped
1 stalk celery, chopped
1 carrot, chopped

## Sauce

125ml (4½ fl oz) white wine
125ml (4½ fl oz) lamb stock

Preheat oven to 180°C / 350°F / Gas 4. Heat olive oil in a large sauté pan. Season racks of lamb with salt and black pepper. When the olive oil is almost smoking hot place the racks, fat side down, in the pan and sear until golden brown.

Remove from pan. Set aside to cool.

To prepare the crust, sauté shallots and garlic in the olive oil until softened. Add breadcrumbs, rosemary, parsley and salt and freshly ground black pepper. Stir and set aside. When the racks have cooled, spread the Dijon mustard over the fat side, then coat with the breadcrumb mixture. Place onion, celery and carrot in a roasting pan and set the racks, breadcrumb side up, on top. Roast for fifteen minutes for medium-rare and twenty to twenty-five minutes for more well done. Remove racks from the oven and set aside in a warm place.

Discard vegetables, pour off all excess fat from the roasting tin and set it over medium-high heat. Deglaze the pan with white wine, scraping up all the bits from the bottom of the pan. Reduce liquid by half, then add lamb stock and reduce for five more minutes, then strain. Slice the racks between the bones, keeping the crust intact.

Divide chops evenly between four plates, overlapping in a semi-circle and spoon a little sauce over each chop.

# Alma-Ata Lamb Pilaf

Serves 6

*450g (1lb) leg of lamb, cut into cubes*
*4 tablespoons vegetable oil*
*2 large carrots, cut into julienne strips*
*2 large onions sliced*
*10 dried apricot halves, chopped*
*⅓ cup raisins*
*1 tablespoon grated orange rind*
*3 cups long-grain rice*
*1¾ cups chicken stock*
*⅔ cup orange juice*
*2½ cups water*
*salt and pepper*
*1 apple, cored and sliced*
*½ cup blanched slivered almonds for garnish*

Sauté the lamb cubes in half the oil over high heat in an ovenproof casserole until brown and there is no liquid left. Remove from casserole and keep warm. Reduce heat and sauté the carrots and onions in remaining oil until lightly browned. Stir in dried apricots, raisins, orange rind and the rice. Sauté until rice is covered with the oil and getting opaque. Add the lamb and stir in the liquids, salt and pepper. Cover casserole and transfer to the oven. Cook for about forty minutes at 180°C / 350°F / Gas 4. Gently stir in the apple slices.

Serve garnished with the blanched slivered almonds.

# Chicken Korma

Serves 4

*4 skinless chicken breasts, each weighing 180g (6oz)*
*4 tablespoons vegetable oil*
*2 cloves garlic, crushed*
*1 large onion, finely chopped*
*2 teaspoons ground coriander*
*½ teaspoon ground cumin*
*1 teaspoon turmeric powder*
*½ teaspoon chilli powder*
*2 teaspoons garam masala*
*2 teaspoons ground almonds*
*200ml (7fl oz) coconut milk*
*100ml (3½ fl oz) single cream*
*salt*
*1 tablespoon chopped coriander leaves*

Cut each chicken breast into four pieces. Heat three tablespoons of the oil in a small sauté pan until very hot. Add the garlic and stir-fry briskly for twenty seconds. Add the onion and reduce the heat. Fry for ten minutes until the onion has softened and caramelized to a golden brown.

Add all the spices and stir-fry quickly for a few seconds then add the ground almonds, coconut milk and cream and cook for five minutes. Take the sauce off the heat and purée in a blender.

Heat the remaining oil in a pan and sear the chicken pieces until golden brown. Add them to the sauce and simmer for fifteen minutes, stirring occasionally, adding a little water for a thick-textured sauce. Salt to taste and sprinkle with chopped fresh coriander leaves.

Serve with basmati rice, cucumber and tomato raita, poppadums or naan bread.

QE2

MEAT, POULTRY AND GAME

# Chicken Tikka Masala

**Serves 4**

*4 skinless chicken breasts,*
*  each weighing about 180g (6oz)*
*4 tablespoons vegetable oil*
*50g (2oz) ginger, finely chopped*
*50g (2oz) garlic, finely chopped*
*1 large onion, finely chopped*
*2 bay leaves*
*3 teaspoons garam masala*
*2 cloves*
*3 whole cardamom*
*3 teaspoons ground coriander*
*2 teaspoons ground cumin*
*1 teaspoon turmeric powder*
*1 teaspoon chilli powder*
*2 teaspoons tomato paste*
*200g (8oz) chopped tinned tomatoes*
*3 teaspoons ground almonds*
*150ml (6fl oz) single cream*
*salt and pepper*
*1 tablespoon chopped fresh coriander leaves*

## Marinade for chicken breasts
*3 teaspoons tandoori paste*
*1 tablespoon lemon juice*
*50ml (2fl oz) plain yoghurt*
*salt and pepper*

Cut each chicken breast into four pieces and mix together all ingredients for the marinade. Add chicken breasts and marinate overnight.

Heat three tablespoons of the vegetable oil in a sauté pan until very hot. Add ginger and garlic. Fry until golden brown, then add onion and sauté until the onion has softened and caramelized. Add bay leaves and all the spices and stir-fry quickly for a few seconds, then add tomato paste and chopped tomatoes. Stir for three to five minutes over low heat, add the ground almonds and the cream and cook for a further five minutes. Remove from heat, take out bay leaves and purée in a blender. Heat the remaining oil in a pan and sear the marinated chicken pieces and add to the sauce. Slowly simmer for fifteen minutes, stirring occasionally and adding a little water if necessary and salt and pepper to taste. Sprinkle with chopped fresh coriander leaves.

Serve with basmati rice, cucumber and tomato raita (chopped cucumber and tomato in yoghurt), poppadums or naan bread.

*QE2*

VIEW · FROM · THE · GALLEY

QE2

# BBQ Braised Short Ribs

Serves 6

2¼ kg (5lb) short beef ribs, trimmed
salt and freshly ground black pepper
3 tablespoons olive or vegetable oil
700g (1½ lb) onions, chopped
250g (½ lb) carrots, cut into chunks
250g (½ lb) celery, chopped
1 head garlic, cut in half lengthwise
6 beefsteak tomatoes, chopped
½ cup tomato paste
8 sprigs thyme
1 sprig rosemary
1 bay leaf
1 cup port
2 cups red wine
1⅛ litres (2 pints) beef stock
2 cups BBQ sauce

Preheat oven to 160°C / 325°F / Gas 3. Rinse the short ribs in cold water. Blot dry and sprinkle with salt and freshly ground black pepper. Heat a flameproof casserole with two tablespoons of olive or vegetable oil over medium heat. Add the short ribs and quickly sear for three to four minutes on each side. Remove from pan. Add remaining tablespoon of oil to the pan and bring almost to smoking point. Add onions, carrots, celery and garlic and sauté until the vegetables are tender. Add tomatoes, tomato paste, thyme, rosemary and bay leaf. Deglaze the pan with port and red wine and reduce for ten minutes. Add beef, beef stock and BBQ sauce. Adjust seasoning with salt and black pepper. Cover and place in the centre of the oven at 160°C / 325°F / Gas 3 for three and a half to four hours or until the meat literally falls off the bone. Using a pair of tongs, remove the short ribs from the sauce and keep warm on a serving dish. Strain the sauce into another pan, discarding the vegetables and herbs and reduce the sauce until it will just coat the back of a spoon. Pour some of the sauce over the meat and serve remainder separately.

A • V E R Y • S P E C I A L • P A S S E N G E R

*Many of the photographs for this book were taken during a Mediterranean cruise – some on the helicopter deck where a rather special passenger had taken up residence: a rare Grey Catbird, the first ever seen in Britain which had got on board on the trip from New York. It was probably blown off course, got tired and dived to the ship for a rest. Second Engineer Malcolm Draper, a keen birdwatcher, spotted and identified it and within hours thousands of enthusiasts had been paged by Rare Bird Alert. Over a thousand people went to Southampton hoping to catch a glimpse of this rare bird (with a cry like a cat's miaow – hence the name). They also hoped that the bird would get off the ship in Southampton, but it was obviously enjoying a life of luxury, being fed biscuits by an attentive crew and stayed on board for the Mediterranean cruise. When the ship got to Malta – this was a Maiden call – what seemed the whole island was waiting to welcome the ship. We stayed in Valetta over night. And by morning the bird had flown – having obviously decided that this was the place to stay.*

# Beef Pot Roast Bourguignonne

Serves 8

2 cups red wine

3 tablespoons olive oil

1 teaspoon salt

1 teaspoon pepper

½ teaspoon ground thyme

1 bay leaf

3 onions

2 carrots

1 celery stalk

3 garlic cloves

1¾ kg (4lb) rump or topside of beef

4 tablespoons butter

¼ cup flour

½ cup beef broth

1 tablespoon tomato paste

1½ cups button onions, par-boiled

¼ teaspoon salt

¼ teaspoon sugar

60g (2oz) sliced mushrooms

Combine red wine, two tablespoons olive oil, salt, pepper, thyme and bay leaf. Slice one onion, one carrot, celery and one garlic clove. Add to wine mixture. Marinate beef in this mixture for at least two hours and up to twenty-four hours, turning it over occasionally.

Remove meat and pat it dry. Strain marinade and reserve. Heat two tablespoons of butter with remaining one tablespoon of olive oil in a heavy frying pan. Brown the meat quickly on all sides. Remove meat to a casserole. Deglaze frying pan with ¼ cup of the reserved marinade and add to meat. Chop remaining onions, carrot and garlic finely. Melt one tablespoon of the butter in a frying pan and sauté the chopped garlic, onions and carrot until lightly browned – about five minutes. Blend in flour and stir for one minute. Add remaining marinade, beef broth and tomato paste. Stir until mixture comes to the boil and pour over meat. Cover casserole with a lid and cook in the oven at 180°C / 350°F / Gas 4 for three and a half hours.

Take the beef out of the sauce and keep warm. Strain the sauce through a fine sieve.

Melt remaining tablespoon butter in a frying pan and sauté the button onions with salt and sugar until golden. Add mushrooms and sauté for two more minutes. Add to the beef and cook for a further ten minutes.

Should the sauce be too thin, reduce and thicken with a little flour or cornflour worked into a knob of butter.

MEAT, POULTRY AND GAME

# Beef Wellington

**Serves 4**

*3 tablespoons butter*
*200g (7oz) shallots, finely chopped*
*400g (14oz) mushrooms, finely chopped*
*salt and pepper*
*1 bunch parsley, finely chopped*
*500g (1lb 2oz) puff pastry*
*1 kg (2lb 4oz) beef fillet*
*200g (7oz) foie gras terrine (tinned)*
*1 egg*

Melt half the butter, add the chopped shallots and fry them gently until translucent. Add the mushrooms, salt and black pepper and fry until all the liquid has evaporated. Stir in the chopped parsley and set aside to cool.

Roll out the puff pastry to hold the meat comfortably. Season meat with salt and pepper and fry in the remaining butter on all sides. Add foie gras terrine to the cooled mushroom mixture. Put some of this mixture on the puff pastry. Lay the beef on top and surround with the remaining mushroom mixture. Fold puff pastry over meat, sealing all edges. Lay the meat parcel, seam side down, on a baking sheet and cover with strips of cut-off pastry trimmings. Brush with lightly beaten egg and bake in a pre-heated over at 220°C / 425°F / Gas 7.

## QE2

T I P S · F R O M · T H E · C H E F S

Karl Winkler says 'The general rule is thirty to forty minutes for medium rare, but as the thickness of the meat can vary considerably, it is best to test after twenty-five minutes with a meat thermometer. Remember: 50°C (122°F) for rare, 54°C (130°F) for medium rare, 60°C (140°F) for medium and 70°C (158°F) for well done. And don't forget that the meat should rest for ten to fifteen minutes before carving.'

# Roast Quail filled with Foie Gras on a bed of Green Lentils with Shallot Confit

**Serves 4**

*100g (3½ oz) fresh foie gras*
*olive oil for frying*
*2 chicken breasts*
*salt and pepper*
*200ml (7fl oz) double cream*
*4 breast-boned quail*
*4 rashers bacon*
*asparagus tips to garnish*

## Green Lentils

*1 onion*
*2 teaspoons butter*
*100g (3½ oz) smoked belly pork, diced*
*300g (11oz) green lentils, soaked for one hour*
*        and drained*
*thyme*
*1 bay leaf*
*salt and pepper*

## Quail Jus

*1 tablespoon finely chopped shallots*
*2 tablespoons butter*
*1 cup port*
*sprig thyme*
*3 cups brown quail stock made with the removed*
*        quail bones*
*salt and pepper*
*shallot confit (see page 90)*

For the stuffing fry the foie gras lightly in a little olive oil to seal. Dice the chicken breasts, put into food processor, add seasoning and blend with cream until smooth. Dice the foie gras and fold in. Stuff the quail with the filling and wrap a bacon rasher around each bird. Roast at 190°C / 375°F / Gas 5 for twenty minutes. On the QE2 the quail are then placed under a hot salamander to crisp the skin. For home use it is best to put them under a grill or turn up the oven heat for a few minutes to achieve the same effect.

To prepare the lentils, dice the onion and sauté in the butter with the diced smoked pork. Add the lentils and cover with water (or chicken stock), add thyme and bay leaf, season and cook for about twenty-five minutes.

To make the jus, sweat the shallots in butter over low heat, add the port and thyme sprig and reduce until the liquid has practically evaporated. Add the quail stock, and reduce to about a quarter, then strain and adjust seasoning.

Serve quail on a mound of lentils, surrounded with quail jus and accompanied by shallot confit. Garnish with asparagus tips.

# Shallot Confit

Yields about 5kg – enough to serve as an accompaniment for 50 main courses – but will keep for months in a cool place.

*3½ kg (about 10lb) shallots*
*1¼ kg (2¾ lb) honey*
*125g (4½ oz) grated ginger*
*salt and pepper*
*280ml (½ pint) wine vinegar*
*280ml (½ pint) water*

Peel the shallots, blanch them for two minutes, strain and refresh with cold water. Melt the honey together with the grated ginger. Add shallots, salt and pepper. Cook slowly until you get a clear caramel. Add the vinegar and water and cook gently, stirring constantly, until reduced to confit consistency. Fill into warm, clean jars and close securely.

### TIPS·FROM·THE·CHEFS

A disc of greaseproof paper dipped into brandy and placed on top of the confit before sealing improves the flavour even further.

# Roast Ducklings à l'Orange

**Serves 4**

2 ducklings each weighing about 2kg (4½ lb)
salt, freshly ground black pepper
4 unsprayed oranges
2 stalks celery, chopped
1 medium-sized onion, chopped
2 cups veal or duck stock
1 lemon
2 tablespoons sugar
2 tablespoons vinegar
2 tablespoons butter
1 cup orange juice
½ teaspoon cornflour
¼ cup Grand Marnier

Prepare the ducklings for roasting by trimming off excess fat, particularly at neck and base end. Rub inside and outside with salt and pepper. Remove zest of unsprayed oranges with a vegetable peeler or lemon zester. Put half the zest into the ducklings. Truss the ducklings and roast them in a pre-heated oven at 220°C / 425°F / Gas 7, for one to one and a half hours, basting occasionally with the pan juices. Remove ducklings from the oven and keep warm on a wire rack. Pour off all but two tablespoons of fat from the roasting pan, add onion and celery and sauté until browned. Add the veal or duck stock and reduce by half.

Cut remaining orange zest into fine long julienne strips, place in a small saucepan, cover with water and bring to the boil. Strain and repeat. Squeeze two of the oranges for juice. Cut remaining oranges into segments for garnish.

Prepare the orange sauce: melt the sugar with a little water in a saucepan and boil over medium heat until it caramelizes. Add orange juice, vinegar and reduced stock and cook until sauce becomes syrupy. Strain the sauce and, if necessary, thicken with cornflour slaked with a little water. Add juice of one lemon and Grand Marnier. Whisk in the butter to give the sauce a nice sheen, then add the blanched orange zest strips.

MEAT, POULTRY AND GAME

QE2

V I E W · F R O M · T H E · G A L L E Y

*On the QE2 the presentation of the Roast Ducklings à l'Orange is rather spectacular: roast duck portions are flambéed with Grand Marnier at the table, orange segments and juice are added and the sauce is finished with a flourish of flames before being spooned on to plates.*

# Pheasant Breast on Savoy Cabbage with Madeira Sauce

**Serves 4**

*4 pheasant breasts including wing bone, skinned*
*salt and freshly ground black pepper*
*2 tablespoons butter*

## Madeira Sauce

*1 shallot, finely sliced*
*1 clove garlic, sliced*
*4 tablespoons butter*
*1 cup dry red wine*
*¼ cup Madeira*
*3 cups brown chicken stock*
*small sprig thyme*
*salt and freshly ground black pepper*

## Garnish

*4 medium-sized Savoy cabbage leaves*
*8 celeriac ovals, trimmed*
*2 tablespoons butter*
*12–14 glazed chestnuts*

To make the sauce, sweat shallot and garlic in a frying pan over low heat with the butter. Add the red wine and Madeira and reduce to half. Add chicken stock and thyme, reduce to one quarter. Season with salt and freshly ground black pepper. Strain and keep hot.

Season and seal the pheasant breasts in butter on both sides in a frying pan. Then transfer to oven and roast at 180°C / 350°F / Gas 4 for ten minutes. They should still be slightly pink in the centre.

Blanch cabbage leaves in salted water. Refresh with cold water and pat dry with kitchen paper. Cook celeriac in salted water until tender.

Sauté cabbage leaves briefly in butter and place in centre of each plate. Toss celeriac in hot butter and arrange on plate. Set the pheasant breast in centre of each plate and surround with Madeira sauce and glazed chestnuts.

# Coq au Vin with Wild Mushrooms

**Serves 4**

2 spring chickens, weighing about 560g
    (1¼ lb) each
flour for coating chicken pieces
2 tablespoons olive oil
3 heaped tablespoons butter
2 tablespoons flour
1 tablespoon tomato paste
3–4 tablespoons brandy
700ml (1¼ pint) full-bodied Burgundy
twigs of fresh rosemary and thyme
salt and freshly ground white pepper
560ml (1 pint) chicken stock

## Marinade

1 medium-sized carrot, diced
2 celery stalks, diced
1 medium-sized onion, diced
4 cloves garlic, chopped
1 bay leaf
5 cloves
20 black peppercorns
1 litre (1¾ pints) full-bodied Burgundy

## Garnish

2 tablespoons butter
225g (8oz) small button onions or shallots
110g (4oz) lean bacon, diced
450g (1lb) wild mushrooms including some morels
50g (2oz) butter blended with 1 tablespoon
    mixed herbs
8 slices bread (heart-shaped or cut from a
    baguette)

Quarter the chickens, removing skin. Combine ingredients for marinade and marinate chicken pieces for twenty-four hours in a refrigerator, making sure that they are completely covered with the wine.

Remove chicken pieces from marinade, pat dry with kitchen paper. Strain the marinade and bring to the boil, skimming off any impurities that rise to the top. Coat the chicken pieces with flour, shaking off any excess flour. Sauté chicken pieces in oil and remove from the pan. Add one tablespoon of butter to pan and sauté vegetables from the marinade until golden brown. Stir in flour and tomato paste and sauté for a few minutes, stirring all the time. Deglaze with brandy and wine, stirring constantly, then add the hot marinade, herbs, seasoning and chicken stock and cook uncovered for thirty minutes. Add the chicken pieces and transfer to an ovenproof casserole. Put into the oven and cook at 200°C / 400°F / Gas 6 for forty to fifty minutes.

Meanwhile melt one tablespoon butter in a frying pan and gently sauté the onions or shallots until caramelized. In another saucepan melt the remaining tablespoon of butter, lightly fry the diced bacon in the butter and add the wild mushrooms. Sauté until mushrooms are cooked.

Remove chicken pieces from casserole and strain the sauce through a fine sieve. Return chicken to sauce, add caramelized onions and mushrooms and simmer for a further ten minutes. Spread the herb butter over the bread slices, set them on a baking sheet and brown in the oven.

# Pink Roasted Venison with Juniper Berry Sauce

**Serves 6**

900g (2lb) rack of venison
salt and pepper
3 tablespoons vegetable oil
6 William pears
½ bottle red wine
½ cup port
½ cup sugar
4 cloves
½ small cinnamon stick
150g (6oz) chanterelle mushrooms
½ teaspoon chopped parsley

## Juniper Berry Sauce

450g (1lb) lean venison trimmings
2 tablespoons and 1 teaspoon butter
110g (4oz) coarsely chopped onions
55g (2oz) coarsely chopped celery
55g (2oz) coarsely chopped carrots
1 teaspoon tomato paste
1 cup red wine
¼ cup Madeira
2 sprigs thyme
1 bay leaf
1 clove garlic
10 black peppercorns, crushed
5 juniper berries
1 quart veal stock
salt and pepper
1 tablespoon red wine vinegar

Sear the venison trimmings in two tablespoons butter, then add onions, celery and carrots and lightly brown them. Add tomato paste, stir and pour in one cup red wine and the Madeira and reduce until almost evaporated. Add thyme, bay leaf, garlic, peppercorns, juniper berries and the veal stock. Simmer for one hour and skim off any fat and impurities that rise to the surface. Strain and adjust seasoning with salt and pepper and vinegar. Reduce to one and a half cups and set aside, keeping it warm.

Trim venison rack and season with salt and pepper. Sear in hot vegetable oil and place in a roasting tin. Roast at 160°C / 350°F / Gas 4 for twelve to fifteen minutes for medium-rare. Remove from oven and keep in a warm place for ten minutes.

Peel and core the pears, leaving the stems on. Poach pears in red wine and port with sugar, cloves and cinnamon.

Sauté the chanterelle mushrooms in butter and season with salt and pepper. Add parsley. To serve, slice venison into single chops and arrange with mushrooms, the poached pears and the sauce on plates.

# An Ocean of Well-being

*C*hefs on the QE2 will cope splendidly with any diet, provided they are given due advance notice. There are some excellent vegetarian main courses on all daily menus and special vegetarian dishes can always be ordered in advance.

If you are truly worried about putting on weight – and five delicious meals a day can be only too tempting – take a look at the daily Spa menus which give calorie as well as fat and sodium counts. In fact, some of the dishes are so tempting that it is no hardship at all to slip in one or the other to balance any over-indulgence – past, present and future and I thought the recipes well worth including. You will notice that salt has not been included in some of the recipes, but this is of course a matter for personal preference.

GOLDEN FRIED MUSHROOM CAPS WITH STILTON,
HERB SAUCE AND CELERIAC PURÉE

## · Vegetarian and Spa ·

Grilled Aubergine Sandwich
with Tzatsiki

Golden Fried Mushroom Caps with Stilton,
Herb Sauce and Celeriac Purée

Fettuccine Primavera

Pappardelle with Sun-dried Tomatoes

Tomato Sauce

Baked Aubergine Parmigiana

Vegetable Paella

Vegetable Strudel with Sweetcorn Sauce

Fruit Pizza with Raspberry Sauce

Garlic Rosemary Baguette Cheese Toasts

Celeriac and Apple Salad
with Grainy Mustard Dressing

Spinach Salad Mimosa

Cucumber filled with Lox and Ricotta

Bouillabaisse Stock

Spa Bouillabaisse

Spa Marinara Sauce

Red Pepper Bisque
with Plum Tomatoes and Saffron

Green Apple, Lime and Candied Ginger
Sorbet

Oven-dried Plum Tomato Dressing

Balsamic Vinaigrette

Spa Pesto

Seared Salmon with Lemon Thyme
and Olive Oil

Chicken Yakitori

Guinea Fowl with Apples and Calvados

Rosewater Angel Food Cake

Spa Apple Strudel

Rhubarb, Apple and Strawberry Compôte
with Orange Meringue

# Grilled Aubergine Sandwich with Tzatsiki

 Serves 4

*4 plum tomatoes, cut in half lengthwise*
*extra-virgin olive oil*
*sugar*
*salt and pepper*
*1 medium aubergine*
*4 pitta breads*
*1 cup diced cucumber*
*½ garlic clove, crushed*
*1 cup Greek yoghurt*
*mint leaves*

Heat oven to 120°C / 250°F / Gas 1–2. Arrange tomatoes on a baking sheet, cut side upwards and brush with extra-virgin olive oil. Sprinkle with sugar, salt and pepper and bake for two hours. The tomatoes should be wrinkly, but still quite juicy. Slice the aubergine into 1cm (½ in) rounds. Brush both sides with extra-virgin olive oil and season with salt and pepper. Grill for about three minutes on each side. Place pitta bread on a baking sheet and warm in the oven at 120°C / 250°F / Gas 1–2. Split open and fill with tomatoes, grilled aubergine and Tzatsiki made by folding diced cucumber and crushed garlic clove into yoghurt, season with salt and pepper. Decorate with mint leaves.

# Golden Fried Mushroom Caps with Stilton, Herb Sauce and Celeriac Purée

ILLUSTRATED ON PAGE 98

 Serves 4

450g (1lb) button mushrooms
salt and pepper
juice ½ lemon
280g (10oz) Stilton cheese
1 cup breadcrumbs
½ cup ground walnuts
½ cup flour
2 eggs
oil for deep-frying

## Celeriac Purée

1 celeriac weighing 225–280g (8–10oz)
1 cup vegetable stock
1 small shallot, peeled and sliced
salt and pepper
1 bay leaf
½ cup crème fraîche

## Herb Sauce

2 cups vegetable stock
1 cup crème fraîche
salt and black pepper
3 tablespoons freshly chopped herbs
        (chervil, tarragon, chives, parsley and basil)

To prepare the celeriac purée, peel the celeriac, dice and cook in vegetable stock with the shallot, seasoning, bay leaf and crème fraîche until tender. Remove bay leaf. Blend in food processor until smooth and keep warm.

To make the herb sauce, reduce the vegetable stock with the crème fraîche until it covers the back of a spoon. Season to taste and add freshly chopped herbs just before serving.

Clean mushrooms and remove stalks. Season mushroom caps with salt, pepper and lemon juice. Stuff mushroom caps with Stilton cheese and smooth over surface. Mix together breadcrumbs and ground walnuts. Dip filled mushroom caps first in flour, then into lightly beaten eggs and finally in the breadcrumb and walnut mixture. Deep-fry in oil and drain on kitchen paper. Serve on top of celeriac purée, surrounded by herb sauce.

QE2

QE2

# Garlic Rosemary Baguette Cheese Toasts

 Serves 20 (3 slices per person)
88 calories per serving

2 tablespoons olive oil
4 tablespoons crushed garlic
1½ teaspoons chopped rosemary
1 tablespoon active dry yeast
1½ cups tepid water
2 teaspoons sugar
1 teaspoon salt
2½ cups white unbleached flour
cornmeal for sprinkling
110g (4oz) Parmesan cheese
vegetable oil spray

Preheat the oven to 180°C / 350°F / Gas 4. Heat oil in a frying pan, add garlic and rosemary. Cover and cook gently for one to two minutes. Set aside to cool. Combine yeast, water, sugar and salt in a large bowl. Set aside in a warm place until yeast begins to bubble. Stir in half the flour. Add the garlic and rosemary mixture. Add remaining flour, a little at a time, kneading the mixture to form a smooth, elastic dough. Form a ball and place in a lightly oiled bowl. Cover and leave to rise in a warm place until doubled in volume. Tip out dough on to a floured board and knead well. Divide dough into three 25cm (10in) long baguettes. Place on oiled baking sheets. Sprinkle cornmeal over baguettes. Leave to rise until about doubled in size. Bake for about forty minutes until crisp and brown.

Remove from oven and set on a rack to cool. Reduce oven heat to 150°C / 300°F / Gas 2. Diagonally cut each cooled baguette into twenty thin slices. Spray baking sheet with vegetable oil spray. Arrange slices on baking sheet sprinkle with grated Parmesan cheese and bake for ten to fifteen minutes until crisp.

# Celeriac and Apple Salad with Grainy Mustard Dressing

 Serves 6  •  41 calories per serving

250g (9oz) celeriac peeled, rinsed and julienne cut
1 tablespoon fresh lime juice
1 tablespoon coarse Dijon mustard
½ cup mustard dressing (see below)
1 green apple, cored and cut into strips
salt
freshly ground black pepper
110g (4oz) lettuce torn into pieces
6 radishes, thinly sliced
2 tablespoons chopped parsley

In a large bowl mix together celeriac, lime juice, mustard and Dijon mustard dressing. Cover and let stand for one hour or more. Add green apple, salt and freshly ground black pepper and toss well. Line plates with torn lettuce pieces. Put mounds of the celeriac mixture in the centre. Garnish with radish slices and sprinkle with chopped parsley.

# Mustard Dressing

Serves 10, Makes 1¼ cup dressing
31 calories per serving

1 tablespoon finely chopped shallots
3 tablespoons apple-cider vinegar
1 tablespoon water
3–4 tablespoons coarse-grain mustard
2 tablespoons corn oil
2 tablespoons honey (optional)

Place all ingredients into a blender and blend well.

# Spinach Salad Mimosa

Serves 6
59 calories per serving

*200g (7oz) fresh spinach leaves*
*½ cup lemon parsley dressing (see below)*
*¼ cup sunflower seeds, toasted*
*3 hard-boiled egg whites*

## Garnish
*¼ cup freshly chopped parsley*
*2 cups alfalfa sprouts*

Put washed and dried spinach into a bowl and dress with lemon parsley dressing. Divide between six plates. Sprinkle with toasted sunflower seeds and chopped hard-boiled egg whites (the yolks are not used for this recipe). Garnish with chopped fresh parsley and alfalfa sprouts.

# Spa Lemon Parsley Dressing

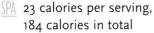

Serves 8
23 calories per serving,
184 calories in total

*½ cup water*
*pinch salt*
*6 tablespoons fresh lemon juice*
*½ teaspoon freshly ground black pepper*
*1 tablespoon corn oil*
*3 tablespoons finely chopped parsley*
*3 tablespoons finely chopped basil or tarragon*

Dissolve salt in water, mix water and lemon juice. Blend together with all the other ingredients.

# Cucumber filled with Lox and Ricotta

Serves 4
61 calories per serving

*1 or 2 cucumbers weighing about 450g (1lb),*
*    skinned and cut into chunks*
*    2cm (¾ in) thick*
*110g (4oz) low-fat ricotta cheese*
*15g (½oz) smoked salmon*
*½ teaspoon horseradish*
*½ teaspoon fresh lemon or lime juice*
*1 teaspoon capers*
*dill sprigs*

Using a melon baller or coffee spoon scoop out centre part of cucumber chunks to make small bowls. Combine ricotta cheese, smoked salmon, horseradish and lemon juice in a food processor and blend until smooth. Pipe into cucumber bowls and garnish with capers and sprigs of dill.

QE2

AN OCEAN OF WELL-BEING

# Bouillabaisse Stock

 Makes about 6 cups (1½ litres/2½ pints)
36 calories per serving

225g (½lb) lobster shells and heads
6 prawn shells and tails
head and bones of sea bass
        weighing about 450g (1lb)
1 stick celery
1 small carrot
1 leek, white part only
2 bay leaves
1 sprig fresh thyme
1 cup loosely packed parsley, whole sprigs
1 teaspoon coarsely cracked peppercorns
12 cups cold water
½ cup dry white wine
salt

Combine all stock ingredients in a large pan.
Bring slowly to just below boiling point – do not
allow to boil. Simmer for about one and a half
hours, skimming surface as necessary, to reduce
to half. Strain and refrigerate if not using
immediately.

# Spa Bouillabaisse

 Serves 6
150 calories per serving

6 cups bouillabaisse fish stock (see left)
2 teaspoons fresh garlic cloves, crushed
1 cup celery, cut into julienne strips
1 cup leek, white part only,
        cut into julienne strips
¼ cup red pepper, cut into julienne strips
¼ cup julienne cut carrots
¼ cup finely sliced fennel
1 cup Marinara sauce (see page 105)
pinch saffron
6 prawns
8½ oz (240g) sea bass, cut into large pieces
5oz (140g) clams, with shell
1 large piece lobster meat with shell, weighing
        about 100g (3½ oz)
dash of Pernod
¼ cup parsley, finely chopped

To make the bouillabaisse, bring one cup of the
fish stock to the boil. Add garlic, celery, leeks, red
pepper, carrots and fennel. Simmer for five
minutes. Add Marinara sauce, saffron and the
remaining fish stock. Simmer for ten to twelve
minutes. Add prawns, sea bass, clams and lobster.
Simmer for about three to four minutes, until
fish is just done. Add Pernod, parsley and thyme.
Serve immediately.

# Spa Marinara Sauce

 Makes about 3½ cups sauce
total calories 470

1 teaspoon olive oil
1 small onion, chopped
4 garlic cloves, crushed
900g (2lb) tomatoes, peeled, seeded and diced
     (or canned)
1 cup tomato paste
2 teaspoon fresh thyme, finely chopped
1 tablespoon fresh oregano, finely chopped
1 bay leaf
1 teaspoon sugar (optional)
1 cup basil leaves, cut into strips
freshly ground black pepper to taste

Heat the olive oil in a medium-sized saucepan.
Add onion and garlic and sauté until soft. Add
tomatoes, tomato paste, thyme, oregano, bay leaf
and sugar. Cook for approximately forty-five
minutes over medium heat, stirring occasionally,
until thickened. Remove bay leaf, add basil strips
and freshly ground black pepper.

# Red Pepper Bisque with Plum Tomatoes and Saffron

 Serves 6
85 calories per serving

1 tablespoon olive oil
1 large onion chopped
1 garlic clove, crushed
340g (12oz) plum tomatoes peeled and seeded
4 large red peppers, charred, peeled and seeded
1 bay leaf
4½ cups vegetable stock, or fat-free chicken stock
pinch saffron
fresh basil or chervil sprigs for garnish

Heat olive oil in a large saucepan. Add onion
and garlic. Cover and cook gently for a few
minutes. Add tomatoes and simmer for about ten
minutes. Add peppers, bay leaf and stock.
Simmer for about forty minutes. Remove bay
leaf and leave to cool. Transfer to food processor
or blender and pulse a few times. Do not over
process. Strain through a fine sieve. Add saffron,
re-heat gently and serve garnished with sprigs of
basil or chervil.

# Green Apple, Lime and Candied Ginger Sorbet

 Serves 4
90 calories per serving

350g (12½oz) green apples (Granny Smith, Pippin
    or Gravenstein) peeled, cored and thinly
    sliced
2 cups unsweetened apple juice
1 tablespoon of lime juice
1 tablespoon candied ginger, chopped

### Garnish
50g (2oz) green apples, thinly sliced
4 sprigs mint

Put apples and the two fruit juices into a blender
and process until smooth. Add candied ginger
and blend briefly. Freeze as described on page 49.
Serve garnished with apple slices and sprigs of
mint.

105

# Fettuccine Primavera

 Serves 4

115g (4oz) fresh green asparagus
4 tablespoons butter
¼ cup finely chopped onions
¼ cup finely chopped celery
½ cup finely diced carrots
¼ cup finely diced courgettes
½ cup finely diced red pepper
salt and freshly ground black pepper
1 cup double cream
450g (1lb) dried fettuccine
¼ cup freshly grated Parmesan cheese
2 tablespoons finely chopped flat-leaf parsley

Trim and peel the lower green portions of the asparagus. Cook whole in salted boiling water until tender. Refresh with cold water, drain and cut into 2cm (¾in) lengths. Melt butter in a large frying pan over medium-high heat. Soften onions in the butter for five minutes then add celery and carrots and sauté for another five minutes. Add the courgettes and the red pepper and continue to sauté over medium-high heat until all the vegetables are tender and lightly coloured – ten to twenty minutes, according to the size of the frying pan. Add salt and freshly ground black pepper. Add asparagus and sauté for one minute, then add the cream and cook, stirring occasionally, until the cream has reduced by half. Remove from heat and keep warm.

Bring a large saucepan of water to the boil, add a tablespoon of salt and the pasta, stir so that the pasta does not stick to the bottom of the pan. Cook until the pasta is *al dente*, drain and toss it with the sauce, adding the grated Parmesan cheese and the parsley. Serve at once.

# Pappardelle with Sun-dried Tomatoes

 Serves 4

½ cup extra-virgin olive oil
4 large tomatoes, skinned,
    de-seeded and cut into chunks
1 tablespoon finely chopped garlic
1 cup sun-dried tomatoes in oil
salt and pepper
1 small courgette
450g (1lb) dried pappardelle
2 tablespoons toasted pine nuts
2 sprigs basil, chopped
2 tablespoons flat-leaf parsley, chopped
¼ tablespoon red pepper flakes
½ cup Parmesan shavings
4 basil leaves, deep-fried
¼ cup basil-infused oil (optional)

Heat extra-virgin olive oil in a large frying pan, add tomatoes, garlic and sun-dried tomatoes, drained of oil and sliced into wedges. Simmer gently for ten minutes. Season with salt and pepper. Slice the courgette finely with a mandolin cutter. Blanch in salted water, drain and pat dry. Cook the pasta in salted water until *al dente*. Drain and add to the tomatoes, together with courgettes, pine nuts, chopped basil, parsley and pepper flakes. Adjust seasoning if necessary. Toss together and arrange on pasta plates. Decorate each serving with Parmesan shavings, a crisply fried basil leaf and a sprinkling of basil-infused oil.

# Oven-dried Plum Tomato Dressing

 Makes 2½ cups (40 tablespoons) dressing, 12 calories per tablespoon

670g (24oz) plum tomatoes, halved
2 teaspoons dried thyme
1 teaspoon freshly ground black pepper
2 tablespoons olive oil
1 large shallot, coarsely chopped
1½ cups water
¼ cup balsamic vinegar
½ cup roughly chopped fresh parsley

Arrange tomatoes on a baking sheet. Sprinkle with thyme, black pepper and olive oil. Bake at 120°C / 250°F / Gas 1–2 for about five hours, until juices are no longer apparent when tomatoes are pressed. (There will also be some browning of the juices.) Remove tomatoes from oven and set to cool. Transfer tomatoes to a blender or food processor, add shallot, water and balsamic vinegar and blend until smooth. Add parsley and pulse several times, until parsley is finely chopped.

QE2

# Balsamic Vinaigrette

Serves 8
37 calories per serving

3 tablespoons water
salt
½ teaspoon freshly ground black pepper
¼ cup balsamic vinegar
2 tablespoons Dijon mustard
2 tablespoons olive or vegetable oil

Dissolve salt in water, then add freshly ground black pepper and blend together with all other ingredients.

# Tomato Sauce

 Yields 1½ litres (about 2¾ pints)

1 medium-sized onion, chopped
1 garlic clove, chopped
⅓ cup olive oil
1¾ kg (4lb) tinned Italian plum tomatoes, chopped
½ cup tomato juice
2 tablespoons sugar
½ teaspoon finely chopped oregano
½ teaspoon finely chopped thyme
1 teaspoon finely chopped basil
salt and pepper

Sauté onion and garlic in olive oil without colouring. Add chopped tinned tomatoes with their juice and the tomato juice. Bring to boil and simmer for twenty minutes, stirring from time to time. Add sugar, herbs, salt and pepper and simmer for another five minutes.

# Spa Pesto

 Serves 4
34 calories per serving

1 tablespoon toasted pine nuts
4 garlic cloves
½ cup non-fat yoghurt
¼ teaspoon freshly ground black pepper
salt
¼ cup (packed) basil leaves

Place pine nuts, garlic, yoghurt, freshly ground black pepper and salt into a blender and process to smooth consistency. Add basil and pulse to incorporate. Do not overblend or pesto will become too green!

# Baked Aubergine Parmigiana

 Serves 4

400g (14oz) large tomatoes
thyme, bay leaf, parsley
2 shallots, chopped
1 lightly heaped tablespoon butter
2 cloves garlic
bunch of basil
good pinch sugar
salt and pepper
4 aubergines, thickly sliced
lemon juice
3 eggs
200g (7oz) Parmesan cheese
250g (9oz) flour
1 cup clarified butter

Scald the tomatoes, refresh with cold water and drain. Remove skin and pips and roughly chop the tomatoes. Make a bouquet garni with thyme, bay leaf and parsley. Sweat the shallots in the tablespoon butter, add the chopped tomatoes, the bouquet garni, garlic and chopped basil.

Season with salt and pepper and a good pinch sugar. Cook uncovered in order to reduce the liquid until sauce consistency is reached. Remove bouquet garni and garlic. Keep warm in a bowl over simmering water – if you are a perfectionist you may blend the sauce, but this is not strictly necessary.

Season the aubergine slices with salt and pepper and lemon juice. Whisk together eggs with half the Parmesan cheese. Dip aubergine slices into flour and then soak them in egg mixture for a few minutes. Fry the slices in clarified butter until golden brown on both sides and drain on kitchen paper.

Put a thin layer of the tomato sauce into a baking dish. Place a layer of aubergines on top, then another thin layer of tomato sauce and a sprinkling of Parmesan cheese. Continue layering in this way, finishing with a layer of Parmesan cheese. Bake at 180°C / 350°F / Gas 4 for forty-five minutes.

Serve sliced into portions, accompanied with remaining tomato sauce.

*QE2*

VIEW · FROM · THE · MARKET

QE2

# Vegetable Paella

 Serves 4

2 beefsteak tomatoes, seeded and cut into chunks

3 cloves garlic, peeled and chopped

½ cup chopped parsley

560ml (1 pint) vegetable stock

½ teaspoon saffron

2 artichokes

8 green asparagus spears, blanched

2 red onions chopped

2 shallots cut into wedges

½ cup olive oil

1 green pepper, 1 red pepper, 1 yellow pepper,
    seeded and cut into large chunks

½ chilli pepper

1 leek, diced

1 fennel bulb, sliced

2 stalks celery, diced

2 carrots sliced

½ cup savoy cabbage, shredded

2 cups long grain rice

salt and pepper

2 courgettes, sliced

½ cup frozen sweet corn

1 cup green peas, frozen

slices of tomato and peppers, fennel, asparagus
    spears and about 100g (3oz) blanched green
    beans for decoration

Place tomatoes and garlic into a sauté pan with the parsley and reduce until almost dry. Heat the vegetable stock with saffron and bring to the boil. Trim artichokes and cut into quarters. Peel the asparagus and dice. Reserve the tips. Sweat the onions and shallots in olive oil until well-browned. Add the peppers, chilli pepper, leek, fennel, celery, carrots, Savoy cabbage, artichokes, seasoning and the rice. Stir for a few minutes, then add the saffron stock, little by little as it is absorbed by the rice. About ten minutes before the rice is ready, stir in the courgettes, sweet corn, green peas, asparagus tips and the reduced tomatoes. Arrange the paella in a paella pan and decorate with charcoal-grilled slices of tomato, peppers, fennel, asparagus spears and green beans. If no charcoal grill is available, sear the vegetables in a lightly oiled griddle-pan.

# Vegetable Strudel with Sweetcorn Sauce

 10–12 portions

## Strudel Pastry

*500g (18oz) flour*

*1 egg*

*5 tablespoons sunflower oil*

*salt*

*250ml (9fl oz) warm water*

*extra sunflower oil and flour*

## Filling

*1 large onion, finely chopped*

*3 tablespoons butter, melted*

*2 cups finely chopped carrots*

*½ cup finely chopped celery*

*1 cup finely chopped leeks*

*1 cup fresh green peas*

*1 cup frozen sweetcorn*

*¼ cup chopped herbs (parsley, chives, chervil)*

*½ cup chicken stock*

*salt and pepper*

*½ cup oatmeal*

*3 eggs*

*6 broccoli florets, blanched*

*6 cauliflower florets, blanched*

*1 cup carrot matchsticks, blanched*

## Sweetcorn Sauce

*2 tablespoons finely chopped onions*

*1 tablespoon melted butter*

*1⅛ litres (2 pints) vegetable stock*

*½ cup chopped cauliflower*

*1 cup frozen sweetcorn*

*½ cup peeled and chopped potatoes*

*salt and pepper*

*1 tablespoon chopped herbs*
*        (parsley, chives, chervil, thyme)*

*baby corn for garnish*

To make the strudel pastry, sift the flour on to a pastry board and make a well in the centre. Drop the egg into the well, add sunflower oil and salt. Mix to a soft dough with the water, kneading well until the dough is soft and elastic. Brush lightly with sunflower oil and cover with clingfilm or with a warmed bowl. Leave to rest for half an hour. Cover a large table with a cloth, dust with flour and place dough in the centre. Roll out gently with a rolling pin as far as it will go, then start pulling out the strudel until the pastry is very thin and transparent. Brush very lightly with sunflower oil before filling.

To make the filling, sauté the onion in butter until translucent. Add chopped carrots, celery and leeks and stir. Add fresh green peas and frozen sweetcorn and sauté for one minute, then add herbs and chicken stock. Season to taste, sprinkle in the oatmeal and simmer until well blended. Remove from heat and cool a little. Beat in the eggs, one by one. Place filling on the pulled-out strudel pastry and top with the blanched broccoli and cauliflower florets and matchstick carrots. Tear off any thick pastry edges and roll up the strudel, sealing the edges. Slide strudel on to a buttered and floured baking tray, brush with melted butter or sunflower oil and bake for forty to fifty minutes at 180°C / 350°F / Gas 4. If the top browns too quickly, cover it lightly with buttered greaseproof paper towards the end of the baking time. Serve warm.

To make the sauce, sauté onions in the butter until translucent. Add the vegetable stock, cauliflower, sweetcorn and potatoes. Simmer for twenty minutes, then season with salt and pepper. Blend in a food processor until slightly chunky and stir in the herbs. Serve with the vegetable strudel and garnish with baby corn.

VEGETABLE STRUDEL WITH SWEETCORN SAUCE

# Seared Salmon with Lemon Thyme and Olive Oil

 Serves 6
104 calories per serving

1 tablespoon fresh thyme, chopped
3 tablespoons lemon or lime juice
1 tablespoon olive oil
1 teaspoon freshly ground black pepper
6 salmon fillets weighing about 170g (6oz) each
vegetable oil spray
lemon wedges for serving

Heat a griddle pan. Combine thyme, lemon juice, olive oil and pepper in a mixing bowl. Place the salmon fillets in the bowl, ensuring that they are totally covered. Spray the griddle pan with vegetable oil. Sear the fillets on both sides until cooked but still moist inside. Garnish with lemon wedges.

# Chicken Yakitori

 Serves 4
128 calories per serving

1½ teaspoons low-sodium soy sauce
½ teaspoon Saké (rice wine)
½ teaspoon Mirin
⅛ teaspoon crushed fresh ginger root
¼ teaspoon crushed garlic cloves
¼ teaspoon black sesame seeds
4 chicken breasts weighing, 100g–110g
    (3½–4oz) each, skinned
2 tablespoons vegetable stock

Combine the first six ingredients in a small bowl. Place the chicken breasts in a shallow dish, pour the marinade over and leave for approximately one hour. Sear the chicken breasts in a hot griddle pan on both sides, then place them in a shallow baking dish and cover with about two tablespoons vegetable stock. Place in the oven for fifteen to twenty minutes at 240°C / 475°F / Gas 9 until thoroughly cooked.
    Serve with stir-fried vegetables.

# Guinea Fowl with Apples and Calvados

**SPA** Serves 6
227 calories per portion

6 guinea fowl breasts with wings
110g (4oz) onions, cut into large dice
55g (2oz) carrots, cut into large dice
55g (2oz) celery, cut into large dice
4 tablespoons unbleached white flour
2 tablespoons tomato paste
1 cup Cabernet Sauvignon
6 cups vegetable stock or degreased chicken stock
1 heaped teaspoon cornflour
3 tablespoons Calvados
1 Gala apple cut into 6mm (¼ in) thick slices
1 tablespoon cranberry sauce to garnish

## Marinade

¼ cup white wine
1 tablespoon balsamic vinegar
2 tablespoons coarsely chopped shallots
1 tablespoon chopped thyme
¼ teaspoon freshly ground black pepper

Remove wings from the guinea fowl breasts and set aside. Place the breasts, skin side up, in a shallow baking dish.

Combine the white wine, balsamic vinegar, shallots, thyme and freshly ground black pepper and pour over the breasts. Marinate for two to three hours or overnight, if possible.

Place the wings in a shallow baking dish. Roast at 190°C / 375°F / Gas 5 until partially browned. Add the onions, carrots and celery and continue to roast until well-browned. Remove from the oven and drain off fat. Toss the browned wings and vegetables in the flour, add tomato paste and return the dish to the oven to roast for a further fifteen minutes. Transfer wings and vegetables to a saucepan. Deglaze baking dish with the wine, scrape up all the sediments from the bottom of the dish, and add to wings and vegetables in the saucepan. Add vegetable or chicken stock to cover contents of the saucepan. Bring to boil and then simmer – without a lid – to reduce by more than half, skimming off fat and impurities as they rise to the top. Strain through a fine sieve and continue cooking until about one and three quarter cups of liquid is left. Dissolve cornflour in a little cold water and add to liquid. Simmer until thickened. Add Calvados just before serving and adjust seasoning.

Remove guinea fowl breasts from marinade and roast at 190°C / 375°F / Gas 5 for approximately twenty-five to thirty minutes. Sear the apple slices in a hot griddle pan and serve with the guinea fowl breasts, garnished with cranberry sauce and accompanied by the Calvados sauce.

# Fruit Pizza with Raspberry Sauce

 Makes 6 small pizzas or 1 large pizza

## Sweet Yeast Dough

*25g (1oz) fresh yeast*
*100g (3½ oz) caster sugar*
*250ml (9fl oz) tepid milk*
*600g (21½ oz) strong flour*
*pinch salt*
*2 eggs*
*little grated lemon rind*
*125g (4½ oz) butter, melted*

## Custard Pastry Cream

*375ml (13½ fl oz) milk*
*½ split vanilla pod*
*3 egg yolks*
*75g (3oz) granulated sugar*
*50g (2oz) flour*
*2 tablespoons Kirsch*

## Topping

*¼ cantaloupe or honeydew melon*
*⅓ pineapple*
*½ papaya*
*½ mango*
*2 kiwi fruits*
*1 peach*
*2 plums*
*50g (2oz) dark grapes*
*100g (3½ oz) strawberries*
*50g (2oz) blueberries*
*chopped pistachio nuts and mint leaves*
*for decoration*
*Raspberry Sauce (see page 143) and ice-cream*
*to serve*
*75g (3oz) firm apricot jam*

To make the yeast dough, cream the yeast with a teaspoon of the sugar, add half a cup of the tepid milk and sprinkle a teaspoon of the flour over the top. Leave to stand in a warm place to prove (ferment). Sift remaining flour into a bowl with the salt, make a well in the centre, add the remaining milk and sugar, the eggs, lemon rind, melted butter and fermented yeast. Mix well and beat dough with a wooden spoon or the dough hook of an electric mixer until it leaves the sides of the bowl clean. Dust dough with flour, cover with a cloth and leave dough to rise in a warm place until it has increased by a third in volume.

Whilst the dough is rising make the custard pastry cream: bring milk to boil with split vanilla pod. Whisk together egg yolks and sugar, stir in the flour. Gradually pour boiling milk on to the egg yolk mixture, stirring with a small whisk, then pour the mixture back into the rinsed-out saucepan. Cook until thickened, stirring constantly, Remove from heat and stir in the Kirsch. Remove vanilla pod, leave to cool before use.

Knock the dough back and divide into six equal portions. Place on a floured board, dust lightly with flour and allow to rise again.

Flatten dough into circles measuring about 16cm (6in) in diameter, with the rim slightly higher than the centre. Place on buttered and floured dough baking sheet. Fill centre with cooled pastry cream and cover with sliced fruit. Leave to rise again for ten to fifteen minutes.

Bake at 180°C / 350°F / Gas 4 for twenty-five to thirty minutes. Remove from oven and whilst still warm, brush with apricot glaze made by cooking the apricot jam briskly with a tablespoon of water and then sieving it.

Serve pizzas sprinkled with chopped pistachio nuts and decorated with mint leaves, accompanied by raspberry sauce and ice-cream.

AN OCEAN OF WELL-BEING

QE2

AN OCEAN OF WELL-BEING

# Rosewater Angel Food Cake

12 portions
120 calories per serving

1 cup unbleached flour, sifted twice
1 cup sugar
12 egg whites (about 1½ cups) at room temperature
½ teaspoon salt
1 teaspoon cream of tartar
2 teaspoons rosewater
1 teaspoon vanilla extract

Preheat oven to 180°C / 350°F / Gas 4. Sift the flour with half the sugar. Beat egg whites at low speed for one minute. Add salt, cream of tartar, rosewater and vanilla. Beat until mixture is frothy. Increase speed to high and while beating gradually add remaining sugar in a steady stream. Beat egg whites to a soft peak – do not overbeat. Remove beater from mixing bowl and sift half a cup of the flour/sugar mixture over the beaten egg whites and gently fold in. Sift and gently fold in remaining flour/sugar mixture. Pour batter into an ungreased 23cm (9in) savarin tin with removable bottom. Bake for forty-five minutes without opening the oven door. To check whether cake is ready, press the top with your finger – the top should feel firm to the touch and spring back when you lift your finger. If necessary, bake for another five to ten minutes. Remove cake from oven, invert on to a tray and allow to cool.

# Spa Apple Strudel

Serves 8
147 calories per serving

670g (24oz) apples (Gala or Golden Delicious),
        peeled, cored and sliced (about 6 apples)
1–2 teaspoons ground cinnamon
pinch ground cloves
⅓ cup raisins, plumped and drained
¾ cup brown sugar
vegetable oil spray
5 sheets filo pastry, 30cm x 43cm (12in x 17in)
icing sugar

Mix together apple slices, cinnamon, cloves, raisins and brown sugar. Lightly coat a non-stick pan with vegetable oil spray and sauté the apple mixture for eight to ten minutes or until the apples begin to soften. Transfer to a bowl and leave to cool. Spread a sheet of filo pastry on a work surface and spray with vegetable oil spray. Cover with another sheet of pastry and continue stacking and spraying until all five sheets have been stacked. Place cooled apple mixture down the centre and roll up the pastry. Secure openings and place roll – seamed side down – on to a well-sprayed baking sheet. Spray over top of the roll and bake at 180°C / 350°F / Gas 4 for thirty-five to forty minutes.

Serve warm, sprinkled with icing sugar.

# Rhubarb, Apple and Strawberry Compôte with Orange Meringue

SPA  Serves 8 • 193 calories per serving

*8 medium stalks rhubarb,*
*trimmed and cut into 2½cm (1in) pieces*
*2 cups thinly sliced, peeled and cored red apples*
*1 pint (560ml) strawberries,*
*trimmed and thinly sliced*
*¼ cup unsweetened apple juice*
*1¼ cup light-brown sugar*
*1 cinnamon stick*

## Orange meringue
*4 egg whites*
*pinch salt*
*⅓ cup orange-juice concentrate, defrosted*
*icing sugar and 8 raspberries to garnish*

Combine all the fruit, apple juice, sugar and cinnamon stick and cook, covered, stirring occasionally, for ten to fifteen minutes, until slightly thickened. Remove cinnamon stick and allow to cool. Divide between eight small shallow dishes.

To make the meringue, whisk egg whites with a pinch of salt to soft-peak stage. Gradually add the orange-juice concentrate and whisk until thick and smooth. Put mixture into an icing bag with a large nozzle and pipe evenly over the fruit compôte – or spoon it over. Serve immediately, with a sprinkling of icing sugar and a raspberry in the centre.

AN OCEAN OF WELL-BEING

QE2

# Parties, Buffets and Special Events

There is a permanent air of festivity about the QE2 starting with the Captain's party at the beginning of each cruise, when everybody is invited to Champagne and canapés and dress is stictly formal ('the QE2 is the only place where I can still enjoy wearing my jewellery – and feel safe') to the pleasantly brash – and definitely informal – Bavarian Frühschoppen in the butchery on Deck 7: beer and Schnapps, massive hams and sausages and huge apple strudel. And music to match the mood. Not exactly elegant, but great fun. And great food.

Holidays – national and otherwise – are duly celebrated in style, from Hallowe'en (with prizes for the best costume) to Burns Night. The Midnight Buffet is of course a nightly fixture – a perfect meeting place to round off the day – but at least once during every cruise it is replaced by a magnificent Gala Buffet which takes about three days to prepare.

On World Cruises in particular passengers like to hold their own private parties – small ones in their suites or taking over one of the larger venues on the ship – and the food provided is always spectacular with the Chefs dreaming up new culinary delights.

QUEEN ELIZABETH 2 AT VALETTA, MALTA G.C.

## · Parties and Buffets ·

Prawn Cocktail
Sauce for Prawn Cocktail
Eggs Stuffed with Prawns
QE2 Pâté de Campagne
Potato Salad
Beefsteak Tartare QE2

# Prawn Cocktail

### Serves 10

800g (1³/₄lb) raw king prawns
1 litre (1¾ pints) fish stock
250g (9oz) celery
1 lettuce
400g (14oz) tomatoes
1 avocado
400ml (14fl oz) prawn cocktail sauce
100ml (3½ fl oz) double cream
salt and pepper
Tabasco sauce

Peel the prawns and remove black thread. Poach prawns in fish stock and leave to cool in the stock, then cut into pieces. Chop celery. Reserve ten inner lettuce leaves for garnish and cut remainder into strips. Peel tomatoes, deseed and cut into dice. Peel avocado and cut into dice, leaving half for garnish. Put shredded lettuce into individual cocktail glasses or into one large bowl. Mix together prawns and celery. Put half the diced avocado and diced tomatoes with the cocktail sauce. Whisk cream to soft peaks and fold in. Season with salt, pepper and Tabasco.
        Put prawns and celery on top of lettuce and

spoon the cocktail sauce over. Garnish with reserved lettuce leaves, avocado and tomato.

# Sauce for Prawn Cocktail

### Makes 1 litre (1³/₄ pints)

600g (21½ oz) mayonnaise
250ml (9 fl oz) tomato ketchup
100g (3½ oz) low fat Quark
30g (1 generous oz) freshly grated horseradish
2–3 tablespoons brandy
salt
Tabasco sauce
lemon juice

Mix together mayonnaise and tomato ketchup, beat in the Quark and freshly grated horseradish. Add brandy, salt, lemon juice and Tabasco sauce.

# Eggs Stuffed with Prawns

### Serves 10

10 hard-boiled eggs
300g (11oz) cucumber
50g (2oz) fresh dill
300g (11oz) cooked and shelled prawns
100g (3½ oz) mayonnaise
150g (5½ oz) natural yoghurt
salt and pepper
dash lemon juice
sprigs dill for garnish

Halve the eggs, remove yolks, chop and reserve. Peel cucumber, remove seeds and grate. Finely chop the dill. Mix together prawns, yoghurt, mayonnaise, chopped dill and cucumber. Season with salt, pepper and a dash of lemon juice. Pile mixture into egg halves, sprinkle with chopped egg yolk and decorate with sprigs of dill.

# Canapés

Jumbo prawns gently poached in a court bouillon, then chilled. Baguette slices toasted with garlic butter until crisp, spread with a tomato, avocado, cilantro and lime juice relish and topped with halved prawns.

Terrine of foie gras cut into slices and placed on top of toasted brioche. Garnished with a slice of caramelized pineapple and a small wedge of fresh fig.

Sevruga Malossol caviar placed into small red potatoes, previously cooked until just tender, on top of a spoonful of crème fraîche.

Smoked salmon and sturgeon: thinly sliced smoked salmon and sturgeon are arranged alternatively in a circle on a 6mm (¼ in) slice of cucumber. Garnished with watercress, slices of pickled ginger and a few slivers of lemon zest.

Carpaccio of beef garnished with shaved Parmesan cheese, black pepper and extra-virgin olive oil.

Peppered Italian ham wrapped around scoops of cantaloupe or honeydew melon, previously marinaded in port wine, sprinkled with a chiffonade of basil.

Gorgonzola Tartlets garnished with sliced pear, grapes and chives.

Pesto shrimp and fresh mozzarella salad with black olives, roasted garlic and balsamic vinegar served in a cherry tomato.

# Hot Canapés

Chicken roulade: chicken breast stuffed with sautéed red cabbage, apples and toasted pinenuts, rolled up and breaded in Japanese breadcrumbs. The roll is then seared and baked in the oven, sliced and served on toasted bread garnished with apple chutney and thinly sliced red cabbage.

Skewered garlic beef tips first marinaded with roast garlic, olive oil and thyme, then skewered with red and yellow peppers and red onion. Grilled and served with a spinach, cucumber, aubergine, potato and yoghurt dip.

Sesame grilled prawns with pineapple salsa, coconut and cilantro.

Beef Satay with spring onion, spicy pepper and peanut sauce.

Crunchy crab spring rolls: crab meat, Monterey Jack cheese and red pepper rolled into spring wrappers and fried until golden brown, served with sweet chilli sauce.

Goat cheese triangles: a mixture of goat cheese, Pernod, spinach and ricotta cheese is placed into filo dough and folded to form triangles, then baked until golden brown.

A SPECTACULAR QE2 BUFFET

# QE2 Pâté de Campagne

2 pâtés

2 cups fresh breadcrumbs
¾ cup double cream
225g (½ lb) well-chilled fresh pork fat cut into
        2½cm (1in) cubes
350g (¾lb) chicken livers, trimmed
2 eggs
1 medium-large onion, finely chopped
2 large garlic cloves, crushed
1 tablespoon salt
2 teaspoons freshly ground pepper
2 teaspoons ground allspice
1 teaspoon each ground ginger, dry mustard,
        ground thyme and rosemary
½ cup each brandy and Calvados
450g (1lb) veal, minced twice
450g (1lb) pork, minced twice
1 cup shelled, unsalted pistachios
700g (1½ lb) thickly sliced bacon
4 large bay leaves

Combine breadcrumbs and cream in a bowl and
set aside. Put the pork fat in a food processor and
finely chop. Transfer to a large bowl. Process the
chicken livers and add to the pork fat. Whisk
together eggs, onion and garlic. Whisk in the
salt, pepper, allspice, ginger, mustard and herbs,
stir in the brandy and Calvados.

Add the minced veal and pork to the chopped
pork fat and livers. Mix with your hands until
well blended. Mix in the breadcrumbs and cream,
then blend in the egg mixture. Stir in the
pistachios until evenly distributed.

Preheat the oven to 180°C / 350°F / Gas 4.
Line two 23cm x 12½cm x 2½cm (9in x 5in x
1in) loaf tins crosswise with the sliced bacon,
leaving some to overhang on each side and
reserving four strips for the tops. Fill the tins
with the meat mixture, pressing it evenly into the

corners. Fold the bacon over the tops of each
pâté and arrange two bay leaves on each. Top
with the reserved bacon slices. Cover the tins
with double thickness of foil and stand them in a
deep roasting tin. Pour in enough hot water to
reach three-quarters of the way up the tins. Bake
for one hour forty-five minutes or until a knife
inserted into the pâté comes out clean.

Remove the tins from the roasting tin, peel
off the foil and allow pâtés to cool. Cover them
with clingfilm and place one on top of the other.
Place two 400g (14oz) tins on top of the
uppermost pâté and refrigerate, weighted, for two
days. (They can be prepared a week ahead, but
remove the weights after two days.) Unmould the
pâtés and scrape off all surrounding fat. Remove
the bay leaves, leaving the bacon if desired. Slice
and serve slightly chilled.

# Potato Salad

Serves 10

2½ kg (5½ lb) potatoes, unpeeled
1 tablespoon salt
200g (7oz) onions, finely chopped
400ml (14fl oz) beef bouillon
salt and pepper
100ml (3½ fl oz) herb vinegar
200ml (7fl oz) sunflower oil
2 tablespoons finely chopped chives

Cook or steam potatoes in salted water. Peel
whilst still warm and cut into slices. Sprinkle
onions over potatoes and pour the hot bouillon
over them. Dissolve salt in vinegar and whisk in
sunflower oil and pepper to make a vinaigrette.
Pour vinaigrette over the potatoes and mix very
gently. Leave for an hour, gently turning the
potatoes from time to time. Sprinkle with
chopped chives before serving.

QE2

# Beefsteak Tartare QE2

Miniature Steak Tartare are often served as canapés on small rounds of toast at cocktail parties.
10 portions if served as a first course

*500g (18oz) finely chopped or minced beef fillet*
*1 finely chopped small onion*
*20g (⅔oz) chopped capers*
*2 chopped pickled cucumbers*
*8 chopped anchovy fillets*
*1 teaspoon each ground caraway seeds,*
*      salt, pepper, paprika and mustard*
*4 egg yolks*
*a little chopped parsley or chives*

Lightly beat the egg yolks and then work to a
smooth paste with all the other ingredients,
except the meat. Blend the paste into the meat,
work together thoroughly and adjust the
seasoning if necessary. 'A dash of brandy further
improves the flavour,' says Karl Winkler. Shape
into small rounds and garnish with strips of red
or green pepper and/or slices of tomato and
hard-boiled eggs and parsley or chive's.

PARTIES, BUFFETS AND SPECIAL EVENTS

# The Captain's Table

*There are two Captain's Tables on the QE2 – in the Caronia as well as in the Mauretania restaurant and the Captain and the Staff Captain alternate between them. On World Cruises – on nights at sea – the arrangement is different: the Captain's Table in the Caronia restaurant is set for forty and passengers dine there by special invitation.*

*The menu is special as well – a six-course dinner often featuring new dishes that may be incorporated into the other restaurant menus at a later date.*

## Chilled Fennel Essence with Pernod

### Serves 4

*1¾ litres (3 pints) strong beef consommé*
*2 fennel bulbs, diced*
*3 leaves gelatine, soaked in cold water*
*60 ml (2fl oz) Pernod*
*½ cup finely diced fennel, blanched, for garnish*
*salt and pepper*
*½ teaspoon fennel seeds*

Heat the consommé, add the diced fennel and simmer for one hour. Strain, add soaked and squeezed-out gelatine and the Pernod. Adjust seasoning and chill.

Serve chilled – on a bed of crushed ice if possible – garnished with the finely diced fennel.

## Peach and Champagne Sorbet

### About 20 scoops

*500g (18oz) caster sugar*
*500ml (18fl oz) water*
*500g (18oz) fresh ripe peaches, skinned and stoned*
*750ml (27fl oz) Champagne*
*juice 1 lemon*

Dissolve sugar in water, bring to boil and simmer for five minutes. Allow to cool. Cut up the peaches, add enough of the syrup to barely cover and simmer until fruit is soft. Allow to cool. Purée in a processor, add remaining sugar syrup, Champagne and lemon juice then freeze as described on page 49.

# Porcini Risotto with Seared Quail and Parmesan Cheese, Roasted Onions and Pancetta

**Serves 4**

*4 large quail, boned, weighing about 200g (7oz)*
*each*
*4 garlic cloves, sliced thinly*
*8 lemon slices*
*2 tablespoons extra-virgin olive oil*
*1 teaspoon black pepper*
*1 tablespoon rosemary, chopped*
*sea salt*

## Porcini Risotto

*4 cups chicken stock*
*4 tablespoons butter*
*2 tablespoons diced onions*
*salt and pepper*
*1½ cups vialone nano or arborio rice*
*1 cup white wine*
*4 tablespoons dried porcini mushrooms, crumbled*
*2 tablespoons grated Parmesan cheese*
*1 tablespoon chopped chives*

## Garnish

*4 tablespoons pancetta cut into lardons*
*½ cup sliced red onion*
*1 teaspoon sugar*
*1 teaspoon fresh thyme*
*salt and pepper*
*1 cup sliced fresh porcini mushrooms*
*½ cup chicken stock*
*Parmesan shavings*

## · The Captain's Table ·

Chilled Fennel Essence with Pernod

Peach and Champagne Sorbet

Porcini Risotto with Seared Quail
and Parmesan Cheese, Roasted Onions
and Pancetta

Basic Brown Veal Jus

Oven-baked Medallions of Veal
in a Herb Crust

Bitter Chocolate Terrine
with Mocha Sauce

Almond Tuiles

Lemon Sabayon

Warm Chocolate Cake

Crème Anglaise

QE2

Marinate the boned quail with the sliced garlic, lemon, oil, pepper and rosemary. Refrigerate overnight. Season with salt prior to cooking.

To make the risotto, heat a heavy saucepan over medium heat. In another saucepan, heat the chicken stock. Put a tablespoon butter into the first saucepan and when it froths up, add diced onions and season. Sweat over low heat until they are translucent. Add the rice and stir so it is covered with butter. Deglaze with the white wine and simmer until liquid has been absorbed. Add one cup of the chicken stock – to cover – and crumbled porcini mushrooms. Stir over low heat until liquid has been absorbed. Repeat process until all the chicken stock has been absorbed. Add remaining butter and the Parmesan cheese. Adjust seasoning and finish off with chopped chives.

Sweat the pancetta over medium heat, starting off in a cold pan, until the fat starts to run. Fry until crisp. Remove with a slotted spoon and dry on kitchen paper. Reserve some of the rendered fat, retaining about a tablespoon and add the sliced onion. Add a pinch of sugar, thyme leaves, salt and pepper. Caramelize onions over higher heat to colour, but still be crunchy. Remove onions with a slotted spoon and set aside. Heat reserved fat over a high heat and sauté the porcini mushrooms until brown. Season and set aside.

Sear the boned quail in extra-virgin olive oil over high heat until golden brown on all sides, then cook for a further two minutes or until cooked through. Keep warm. Add mushrooms and onions to the pan and deglaze with chicken stock. Place the risotto in a bowl and arrange onion mixture on top. Arrange quail in centre and garnish with Parmesan shavings and pancetta.

# Basic Brown Veal Jus

*3lb (1¼ kg) veal bones and trimmings cut small*
*2 tablespoons olive oil*
*1 onion, diced*
*2 carrots, diced*
*parsley stalks*
*2 twigs fresh thyme*
*1 bay leaf*
*4 cloves garlic*
*1 tablespoon tomato paste*
*¼ litre (9fl oz) white wine*
*3 litres (5 pints) veal stock*

Preheat the oven to 220°C / 425°F / Gas 7. In a large baking dish toss the bones and trimmings in the oil and then roast them until evenly browned. Add the vegetables and garlic, and then roast for another five minutes.

Transfer baking dish to the top of the stove and add the white wine. Reduce to half, then add the veal stock and herbs, bring to the boil and simmer for three hours. Strain into a large saucepan and reduce by a further third or until the jus has a nice glossy consistency. Leave to cool and freeze in convenient portions.

KARL MUEHLBERGER AND KARL WINKLER REVIEW MENUS

QE2

# Oven-baked Medallions of Veal in a Herb Crust

**Serves 4**

*8 medallions of veal, cut from the fillet,*
*weighing about 70g (2½–3oz) each*
*salt and freshly ground pepper*
*2 tablespoons olive oil or clarified butter*

## Herb Crust

*2 cups coarsely chopped fresh chervil, parsley,*
*tarragon and basil*
*2 spring onions*
*2 garlic cloves*
*½ cup soft white breadcrumbs*
*150g (5½ oz) softened salted butter*
*freshly ground pepper and a pinch of salt,*

## Polenta

*1⅛ litres (2 pints) chicken stock or water*
*2 tablespoons olive oil*
*300g (11oz) instant polenta*
*100g (3½ oz) mushrooms, sliced*
*1 tablespoon butter*
*1 tablespoon chopped chives or spring onion tops*
*2 tablespoons freshly grated Parmesan cheese*
*salt and pepper*

## Garnish

*8 baby carrots*
*4 broccoli florets*
*16 mange tout*
*4 roasted baby tomatoes*
*butter for tossing vegetables*
*8 tablespoons brown veal jus (see page 128)*
*2oz (50g) cold butter cut into small cubes*
*4 small herb bundles*

Make a herb purée by placing all the ingredients in a food processor and blend to a smooth purée.

Season the medallions and sear them on both sides in oil or butter until golden brown – about two minutes. Set aside to cool. Top each medallion with the herb purée spread evenly to about 6mm (¼in) thick. Bake for ten minutes at 200°C / 425°F / Gas 7 for medium.

Bring the chicken stock or water to simmering point with two tablespoons of olive oil. Remove pot from heat and quickly pour in all the polenta, beating with a whisk or wooden spoon. Return saucepan to heat and cook for five to six minutes over medium heat, stirring constantly. Season with salt and pepper. Sauté the mushrooms in the butter until all the water has evaporated, then add the fresh chives or spring onion tops. Mix the mushrooms with the polenta. Turn out on to a tray and spread evenly to about 2½cm (1in) thick. Leave to cool, then cut eight rounds with a 5cm (2in) cutter. Sprinkle with Parmesan and bake at 200°C / 400°F / Gas 6 until the polenta is hot and the cheese has melted.

Cook the vegetables – except the tomatoes – and then toss with butter. Heat the veal jus and gradually whisk in the diced butter to thicken. Divide vegetables between four plates and place two veal medallions and two polenta rounds on each plate. Swirl the veal jus over the top and garnish with herb bundles and roasted tomatoes.

# Bitter Chocolate Terrine with Mocha Sauce

Serves 8

3 eggs
50ml (2fl oz) Grand Marnier or Cointreau
50g (2oz) sugar
juice and grated zest 1 orange
300g (11oz) bitter chocolate, melted
½ litre (18fl oz) double cream
Almond Tuiles (see below)

## Mocha Sauce

125ml (4½ fl oz) whipping cream
1 teaspoon powdered instant coffee
110ml (4fl oz) Kahlua liqueur

To make the chocolate terrine, whisk together the eggs, Grand Marnier or Cointreau, sugar and orange juice and zest in a bowl over a pan of simmering water until thick and fluffy. Remove from the heat and whisk until cool. Fold in the melted, but not hot chocolate. Whip the cream to soft peaks and fold into cooled mixture. Pour into a loaf tin lined with clingfilm and refrigerate for four hours.

To make the Mocha sauce, whisk the cream until thickened, then stir in the instant coffee dissolved in the Kahlua liqueur.

Cut the chocolate terrine into 3½cm (1½in) slices and serve with Mocha sauce and almond tuiles.

# Almond Tuiles

75g (3oz) icing sugar
75g (3oz) flour
2 egg whites
50g (2oz) melted butter
1 teaspoon almond essence

Combine the dry ingredients, then add to the egg whites and gradually mix to a smooth paste with the melted butter and almond essence. Leave to rest for at least thirty minutes – the mixture can be made in advance and kept in the refrigerator. Spread the mixture in one-millimetre thick rounds on a non-stick baking sheet and bake for two to three minutes at 200°C / 425°F / Gas 8. Remove with a palette knife and twist into tuiles whilst still warm.

# Lemon Sabayon

Serves 4

4 egg yolks
100g (3½ oz) sugar
juice of 2 lemons
zest of 1 lemon, grated
200ml (7fl oz) white wine

Place egg yolks, sugar, lemon juice and white wine in a bowl over simmering water, being careful that the bottom of the bowl does not touch the water. Whisk until frothy and lightly thickened. Serve at once. At the Captain's Table more often than not this is served as an accompaniment to strawberries macerated in Grand Marnier.

# Warm Chocolate Cake

Serves 8–10

*10 eggs*
*380g (13½ oz) bittersweet chocolate,*
*        broken into pieces*
*225g (8oz) butter*
*100g (3½ oz) granulated sugar*
*Crème Anglaise*

Separate egg yolks and whites. Put the chocolate into a bowl and set it over a saucepan of simmering water until melted. Remove from heat. Stir in the butter – cut into small lumps – and blend until smooth. Whisk egg whites to a soft peak, then whisk in the sugar until stiff peaks are formed. Beat egg yolks into cooked melted chocolate and fold in the egg whites swiftly.

Pour mixture into a greaseproof-paper lined cake tin and bake at 180–190°C / 350–375°F / Gas 4–5 until a toothpick inserted in the middle comes out with a few moist crumbs attached to it. Serve warm with Crème Anglaise and/or almond ice-cream.

# Crème Anglaise

Serves 4

*½ vanilla pod*
*2 cups milk*
*½ cup caster sugar*
*4 egg yolks*

Scrape the vanilla pod seeds into the milk and place over low heat with the sugar. Put the eggs into a bowl and whisk lightly, just to break them up. Pour a little of the hot milk into the eggs to blend, then add the eggs to the remaining milk and cook gently, stirring constantly, until the mixture will coat the back of a spoon. Remove from heat and strain. If the Crème Anglaise is not being used immediately, pour into a bowl sitting on a bed of crushed ice and refrigerate as soon as it has cooled down.

# Great Guest Chefs

*I*n recent years the QE2 has been host to a number of great Chefs who brought their specialities to all the restaurants on board and gave daily demonstrations as well. Guests have included Chefs from famous restaurants, members of The Club Chef de Chefs (Chefs to Heads of State) as well as members of America's Women Chefs and Restaurateurs, the most prominent being a visit by nine Mâitres Cuisiniers de France. This has been called 'the most star spangled banner in the world' since it encompasses 185 Michelin stars – the nine Mâitres Cuisiniers on board accounted for twelve stars between them! Their charter makes somewhat awesome – if amusing – reading: 'the Mâitre Cuisinier lives in his kitchen' and 'Mâitre Cuisinier must regard his guests as potential friends no matter what their class, position or payment' and 'the title of Mâitre Cuisinier carries with it a moral responsibility' (surely recommended reading for some 'celebrity chefs'). It made for great eating – and some great theatre too. I shall never forget Jean Lameloise demonstrating what he called his grandmother's 'Soup of Red Berries'. 'Excellent cold with a raspberry sorbet, but absolutely splendid in winter served hot – without the sorbet of course.' And grandmother always insisted on using a good Burgundy like a Volnay for this dish!

The QE2's young Chefs responded by staging a great cookery competition which was judged by the French Chefs. The display was absolutely brilliant and passengers had to be constantly restrained from sampling – only by the assurance that the winning dishes would eventually be featured in the QE2 restaurants. (The Mauretania restaurant – at that time the busiest restaurant on board with two sittings – walked away with five out of the nine prizes.)

# Steak Tartare

*From the Rainbow Room, New York*

**10 portions**

*550g (1¼ lb) beef top round,
        trimmed and coarsely ground*
*45 ml (1½ fl oz) olive oil*
*1 tablespoon Dijon mustard*
*1 tablespoon chopped cornichons*
*1 tablespoon chopped capers*
*1 finely chopped shallot*
*1 tablespoon chopped flat-leaf parsley*
*Tabasco sauce*
*Worcestershire sauce*
*Salt and pepper*

## Garnish
*Sevruga caviar*
*chervil leaves*
*toasted brioche triangles*

Mix together all the ingredients, except the meat, until well blended, then work into the meat. Adjust the seasoning if necessary. Shape into rounds, top with caviar and garnish with chervil leaves. Serve with toasted brioche triangles

# Garlic-scented Manila Clams steamed in White Wine

*From Chef Thomas Ferlesch,*
*Café des Artistes, New York*

When Chef Thomas Ferlesch presented his menu at the Chefs' Summit at sea, his instructions to the restaurant staff were 'please also provide soup spoons because the broth is delicious to eat with soup spoon'.

**Serves 10**

*2 cups extra-virgin olive oil*
*½ cup chopped or thinly sliced garlic*
*2 cups chopped shallots*
*2 cups tomato concasse*
*⅓ cup chopped fresh thyme*
*⅓ cup chopped fresh rosemary*
*1 teaspoon red-pepper flakes (or to taste)*
*3¼ kg (7lb) washed and cleaned Manila clams*
*3 cups dry white wine*
*salt, if necessary*
*1 cup coarsely chopped flat-leaf parsley*

Heat one cup extra-virgin olive oil in a large, heavy casserole. Add garlic, shallots, tomato concasse, thyme, rosemary and red-pepper flakes. Sweat gently for five minutes. Add Manila clams and dry white wine and stir with a wooden spoon. Cover with a lid and cook on high heat for approximately three to four minutes, until all the clams have opened up. Discard any that have not opened. Add salt if necessary and remaining extra-virgin olive oil and chopped flat-leaf parsley.

Serve at once in pasta bowls, with coarse country bread.

## · Great Guest Chefs ·

Steak Tartare

Garlic-scented Manila Clams steamed in White Wine

Diane Forley's Sautéed Halibut with Green Swiss Chard, Haricots Verts and Couscous in Tomato Cumin Coulis

RoxSand Scocos's Mogul Lamb Chops with Curried Lamb Jus, Crisp Indian Potato Pancakes, Mint and Coriander Chutney

Banana, Pineapple and Passion Fruit Salad with White Pepper Ice-cream

Red Berry Soup infused with Red Wine and topped with Raspberry Sorbet

Apple and Raisin Streusel

Apricot Three Ways: Apricot Sorbet with Apricots Macerated in Hungarian Apricot Brandy

**MAITRE CUISINIER EMIL JUNG,
AU CROCODILE, STRASBOURG**

PARTIES, BUFFETS AND SPECIAL EVENTS

# Diane Forley's Sautéed Halibut with Green Swiss Chard, Haricots Verts and Couscous in Tomato Cumin Coulis

*From the Verbena Restaurant, New York*

**Serves 4**

*4 portions halibut, each weighing 200g (7oz)*
*olive oil*
*250g (9oz) Swiss chard leaves*
*150g (5oz) haricots verts, blanched,*
*       topped and tailed*
*200g (7oz) celery, blanched and chopped*
*400g (14oz) cooked large-grain couscous*

## Tomato Cumin Coulis

*1 onion*
*2 stalks celery*
*1 red pepper, seeded*
*50ml (2fl oz) olive oil*
*1 teaspoon cumin seeds*
*10 plum tomatoes, skinned and chopped*
*500ml (18fl oz) water*
*2 tablespoons sugar*
*450g (1lb) tinned plum tomatoes, with liquid*
*salt and black pepper*
*lemon juice to serve*

Cut the onion, celery and red pepper into large dice and sweat in the olive oil for about seven minutes until translucent. Add cumin seed and heat to bring out the aroma. Add the chopped, skinned tomatoes and water, bring to boil and simmer for twenty-five minutes. Add the sugar and cook for a further fifteen minutes. Lightly pulse the tinned tomatoes in a food processor, retaining a slightly chunky texture, and add. Season with salt and pepper.

Sauté fish in some olive oil for about five minutes, until golden. In a separate sauté pan, heat some more olive oil and sauté the Swiss chard leaves, then add the haricots verts, celery and couscous.

To serve, ladle the coulis over the vegetables and spoon into a plate. Place the fish on top and squeeze fresh lemon juice over it.

# RoxSand Scocos's Mogul Lamb Chops with Curried Lamb Jus, Crisp Indian Potato Pancakes, Mint and Coriander Chutney

*RoxSand Restaurant & Bar, Phoenix, Arizona*

Serves 6

2 tablespoons powdered ginger

1½ tablespoons cayenne

1½ teaspoons each cinnamon and cloves

½ teaspoon cardamon

3 tablespoons coriander, ground

1 teaspoon black pepper

5 teaspoons salt

675 ml (1¼ pint) yoghurt

juice of 6 limes

1½ teaspoons Tabasco

18 lamb chops, trimmed of fat

kosher salt or sea salt

## Lamb Jus

1 litre (2¼ pints) lamb stock

1 tablespoon olive oil

¼ teaspoon curry paste

1 tablespoon Tabasco

## Chutney

60g (2oz) coriander leaves

1–2 mint leaves (no stems)

1 teaspoon finely chopped garlic

15g (½ oz) finely diced ginger

1 serrano chilli, finely chopped
    (with seeds to taste)

juice and zest of 1 lemon

½ teaspoon salt

450ml (16fl oz) extra-virgin olive oil

## Crisp Indian Potato Pancakes

1 tablespoon mustard seeds

450g (1lb) Idaho potatoes,
    coarsely shredded and placed in iced water

1 onion, chopped

1½ tablespoons cumin

1 teaspoon turmeric

220g (8oz) clarified butter

1 teaspoon kosher salt or sea salt

½ teaspoon pepper

1½ tablespoons crushed curry leaves

3 tablespoons chopped coriander leaves

1 serrano chilli, chopped

Toast the spices, then mix all the ingredients except the salt together and rub into the lamb chops. Leave to marinate overnight. Grill the chops and then sprinkle with salt.

To make the jus, reduce the stock by two-thirds and stir in the oil, curry paste and Tabasco.

For the chutney, purée the ingredients in a food processor, gradually adding the oil.

For the pancakes, sauté the mustard seeds until they pop. Drain and squeeze dry the potatoes. Sauté the onion and spices in a little butter, then add salt, pepper and curry leaves. Cover pan with a lid and sauté until the onion is transparent. Leave to cool. Add coriander leaves, serrano and potatoes – do not break up the potato pieces. Grease a thick frying pan with clarified butter. Use about 2oz (60g) of potato mix for each pancake, cook on both sides, sprinkle with salt and drain on paper towels.

QE2

# Banana, Pineapple and Passion Fruit Salad with White Pepper Ice-cream

*From Vong, New York*

Serves 6

60g (2oz) sugar
250ml (9fl oz) water
1 tablespoon Kirsch
sprig of thyme
8 prunes, stoned
2 bananas
½ pineapple
2 passion fruit, sliced

### Ice-cream
500ml (18fl oz) milk
500ml (18fl oz) double cream
2 vanilla pods
1 teaspoon ground white pepper
10 egg yolks
200g (7oz) sugar

Dissolve sugar in water and bring to boil, with the thyme. Add the prunes. Remove from heat add Kirsch and leave in a covered bowl in the refrigerator overnight.

Cut bananas into four slices lengthways, halve the pineapple piece and remove core, then cut into 3mm (⅛ in) slices. Add to the syrup, then add the passion fruit together with the seeds. Marinate for at least twenty minutes. Serve the fruit salad with scoops of ice-cream.

To make the ice-cream, bring milk and cream slowly to the boil with the vanilla pods and the pepper. Lightly whisk together egg yolks and sugar, pour in the boiling milk and return mixture to a rinsed-out saucepan. Cook over low heat – or in a bain marie – until thickened. Strain and leave to cool, then freeze in the ice-cream maker.

# Red Berry Soup infused with Red Wine and topped with Raspberry Sorbet

*From Maître Cuisinier Jean Lameloise, at Chagny (three Michelin stars)*

Serves 10

500g (18oz) strawberries
500g (18oz) raspberries
200g (7oz) blackcurrants
1 bottle red Burgundy (Volnay, Beaune)
100g (3½ oz) caster sugar
zest of 2 oranges and 1 lemon
juice 2 oranges
500g (18oz) white vineyard peaches
    cut into 1cm (½ in) dice
10 scoops raspberry sorbet
sprigs of mint

Halve the strawberries, then put all the ingredients – except the raspberry sorbet and the mint – into a bowl, stir very gently to mix, then refrigerate for several hours.

To serve, divide berry soup between ten soup plates, top with a scoop of raspberry sorbet and garnish with a sprig of mint.

# Apple and Raisin Streusel

*From Mâître Cuisinier Emil Jung,
Au Crocodile, Strasbourg
(three Michelin stars)*

**Serves 8**

*1kg (2¼ lb) Granny Smith apples
80g (3oz) sugar
100g (3½ oz) raisins
2 teaspoons cinnamon
juice 1 lemon
8 strawberries
8 prunes in red wine*

## Almond Base
*3 egg whites
100g (3½ oz) sugar
100g (3½ oz) ground almonds*

## Streusel
*50g (2oz) sugar
50g (2oz) flour
80g (3oz) butter
50g (2oz) ground almonds
1 teaspoon cinnamon*

To make the almond base, whisk egg whites until stiff, whisk in 30g (1 generous oz) of sugar. Fold in ground almonds and remaining sugar. Set eight baking rings measuring 7½cm (3in) in diameter and 4cm (1½ in) high on a non-stick baking sheet and divide mixture between them or pipe out eight circles of the same size on the baking sheet. Bake at 180°C / 350°F / Gas 4 for twenty minutes.

Peel and core the apples. Cut into 2cm (½ in) cubes and cook on low heat with the sugar, raisins, cinnamon and lemon juice, until just cooked – the apples should still retain their shape. Leave to cool.

To make the Streusel, mix together all the ingredients and form into a lump. Chill for a little while to firm, then grate coarsely on to a baking sheet lined with baking paper. Bake for eight minutes at 200°C / 400°F / Gas 6.

To serve, spoon two spoonfuls of the stewed apple on to each biscuit base and sprinkle the Streusel on top. Heat in the oven for a few minutes – this tastes best when served warm rather than hot – and garnish with strawberries and prunes. Serve with Crème Anglaise.

# Apricot Three Ways: Apricot Sorbet with Apricots Macerated in Hungarian Apricot Brandy

*From Chef Thomas Ferlesch,
Café des Artistes, New York*

**Serves 10**

*1 cup Hungarian apricot brandy (Barack Palinka)
1 cup ready-to-eat dried apricots*

## Apricot Sorbet
*950g (1lb 2oz) frozen apricot purée
1⅛ litres (2 pints) simple syrup (see page 50)
½ cup lemon juice
1 egg white*

Dice the dried apricots very finely and macerate overnight in the apricot brandy. Mix together all the other sorbet ingredients and add to the macerated apricots. Freeze as described on page 49.

# Sweet Indulgence

*P*uddings on board the QE2 are rich and varied – wonderful chocolate
    concoctions, deliciously light baked puddings and of course the flambé
dishes and soufflés for which the QE2 dining rooms are famous. The selection is
truly international – French chocolate terrine, Scottish Cranachan and that great
Austrian classic, Salzburger Nockerl – lofty vanilla-scented peaks – vie for pride of
place with Granny Smith Apple Tart and an elaborate Lemon Roulade.

And if you've ever wondered how Strudel pastry is really made and pulled out
to the correct thinness so that you can read a love-letter through it (it has to
be a love-letter, an ordinary letter will not do), there's a fair chance of learning:
Executive Chef Karl Winkler will show you how to do it in one of his cookery
demonstrations.

# Salzburger Nockerl

**Serves 2**

*2 tablespoons caster sugar*
*3 tablespoons unsalted butter*
*¼ cup milk*
*8 egg whites*
*50g (2oz) icing sugar*
*grated rind ½ lemon*
*½ teaspoon vanilla sugar*
*3 egg yolks*
*1 tablespoon plain flour*
*icing sugar for sprinkling*

Preheat oven to 240°C / 475°F / Gas 9. Put caster sugar and butter into a large flame- and ovenproof dish. Place over medium heat and stir until sugar caramelizes. Add milk, stir and let the sugar dissolve. Set aside to cool. Whisk egg whites with half the icing sugar until they start to stiffen. Add the remaining icing sugar and whisk until very stiff. Add grated lemon rind, vanilla sugar and lightly beaten egg yolks. Fold in the flour. 'This should be done very fast,' says Corporate Executive Chef Karl Muehlberger whose treasured recipe this is.

Form three high pyramids at least 16cm (6in) high – and set them, side by side, in the flame- and ovenproof dish with the milk. Sift icing sugar over the top and bake for eight to ten minutes at 240°C / 475°F / Gas 9. Serve at once, dusted with icing sugar.

SWEET INDULGENCE

QE2

*Karl Muehlberger, Corporate Executive Chef of Seabourn Cunard – gifted creative Chef with a Michelin-starred background – is an amiable chap, generous to a fault with his time, sharing knowledge and precious recipes. He cancelled a long-planned holiday at short notice to join us on board the QE2 to prepare the food for photography, occasionally even standing in as a model – literally lending a hand when a visible arm was required in a picture and often working through the night, testing and scaling down recipes for home consumption. All went swimmingly – no heated arguments, culinary or otherwise. Until it came to the recipe for Salzburger Nockerl – stalwart favourite in QE2 restaurants. Until now the recipe used had been Karl Winkler's – like Karl Muehlberger a native of Salzburg – and their recipes differed considerably. (Well, several pinches of sugar, a flick of flour and a smidgeon of egg white, anyhow). I tried to weigh in – literally – by producing the 'original' recipe, signed, sealed and approved by the Salzburg authorities, but this was unanimously brushed aside. (I was graciously allowed to whip the egg whites though, and later lick the egg whisk.) Eventually we settled on Karl Muehlberger's version. 'It is nearest to the one at the Goldener Hirsch in Salzburg,' said Laurie Evans who had photographed the dish there (and incidentally where Karl Muehlberger did his initial training). I wouldn't be surprised, however, if Karl Winkler's version made a return appearance in the QE2 dining rooms at some time!*

QE2

# Raspberry Tiramisu

**6 portions**

340g (12oz) mascarpone cheese
4 egg yolks
110g (4oz) granulated sugar
110ml (4fl oz) Kahlua liqueur
110ml (4fl oz) double cream, whipped
60 boudoir biscuits
½ cup strong espresso coffee
1 cup milk
1 cup fresh raspberries
30g (1oz) cocoa powder
chocolate sticks for decoration
Kahlua Coffee Sauce
Raspberry Sauce

Soften mascarpone cheese by stirring it with a fork. Whisk egg yolks with the sugar over a pan of simmering water until thick and fluffy. Remove from heat and whisk to cool. Add the softened mascarpone cheese, half the Kahlua liqueur and fold in the whipped cream.

Mix together remaining Kahlua liqueur, coffee and milk. Draw boudoir biscuits through this and use to line an 20cm (8in) oval dish, bottom and sides, or sprinkle with the liquid after the dish has been lined. Spread a third of the mascarpone mixture over the biscuits and place a layer of moistened boudoir biscuits on top. and press down lightly. Spread another layer of mascarpone mixture on top and cover with raspberries, masking them with the mascarpone mixture.

Top with moistened boudoir biscuits and finish with the remaining mascarpone mixture. Refrigerate for two hours – until set. Sprinkle top with cocoa powder and cut into wedges.

Decorate with chocolate sticks and serve with Kahlua coffee sauce and raspberry sauce.

# Raspberry Sauce

**Serves 6**

500g (1lb 2oz) fresh or frozen raspberries
juice of ½ lemon
100g (3½ oz) caster or icing sugar

Purée the raspberries in a blender or food processor. Add lemon juice and sugar and stir until the sugar is dissolved. Strain through a fine sieve to remove seeds. Keep in the refrigerator until ready to use.

# Kahlua Coffee Sauce

**Serves 6**

600ml (21½ fl oz) single cream
30g (1 generous oz) instant coffee powder
6 egg yolks
120g (4½ oz) caster sugar
120ml (4½ fl oz) Kahlua liqueur

Bring cream to boil with the coffee powder. Whisk egg yolks with the caster sugar. Pour boiling cream on to egg yolks, stirring or whisking all the time. Return mixture to rinsed-out saucepan and cook gently for a few minutes stirring all the time – until mixture coats the back of a spoon. (Cautious cooks would use a Bain Marie for this, but this is not strictly necessary, provided you are careful and do not allow the mixture to boil.) Remove from heat and add the Kahlua liqueur.

RASPBERRY TIRAMISU (LEFT)

SWEET INDULGENCE

# Kahlua Sabayon

Serves 4

*4 egg yolks*
*3 tablespoons granulated sugar*
*½ cup Kahlua liqueur*

Whisk yolks and sugar in a stainless steel or copper bowl to blend. Whisk in the Kahlua liqueur. Place bowl over a pan of simmering water (don't let the water touch the bottom of the bowl). Whisk constantly until the mixture is thick and holds its shape when trailed from the whisk. Serve warm or cold. If you want to serve the Sabayon cold, leave to cool over a bowl of ice. Whisk half a cup of whipping cream to soft peaks and fold into the chilled Sabayon.

# Chocolate Almond Pudding

Serves 4

*butter and icing sugar for the dish*
*60g (2oz) chocolate*
*3 tablespoons butter*
*3 tablespoons icing sugar*
*3 eggs*
*2 tablespoons granulated sugar*
*1 cup toasted almonds, finely ground*
*Kahlua Sabayon (see above)*
*1 cup double cream for serving*

Set oven at 180°C / 350°F / Gas 4. Butter a 1¼-litre (2-pint) pudding mould and sprinkle with icing sugar. Break chocolate into small pieces and put into a bowl over a pan of simmering water to melt. Cream butter and icing sugar until light and fluffy. Separate egg yolks and whites and beat yolks gradually into the butter mixture. Stir in the melted, but not hot chocolate. Whisk egg whites to soft peaks, then whisk in the granulated sugar until stiff peaks form. Gently fold egg whites into the chocolate mixture, alternately with the ground almonds. Spoon mixture into the prepared mould and stand the mould in a roasting tin. Pour boiling water into the roasting tin to come halfway up the sides of the mould. Bake for approximately forty minutes – until set. Remove mould from water and allow to cool for five minutes. Invert mould on to a warm platter and turn out the pudding.

Serve warm, topped with Kahlua Sabayon and whipped cream.

# Cranachan (Cream Crowdie)

Serves 6

*65g (2 generous oz) oatmeal*
*600ml (21½ fl oz) double cream*
*120ml (4½ fl oz) whisky*
*420g (15oz) fresh raspberries*
*12 chocolate sticks for decoration*
*6 mint leaves for decoration*

Spread the oatmeal on a baking sheet and toast in the oven until golden brown. Whisk the double cream to soft peaks and fold in the whisky and the toasted oatmeal, reserving a little for sprinkling over the top. Divide half the raspberries between six glasses and cover with half the whipped cream. Place remaining raspberries on top and cover with remaining cream. Sprinkle reserved oatmeal over top and decorate with chocolate sticks and mint leaves.

CRANACHAN (RIGHT)

QE2

# Pancakes Stuffed with Curd Cheese

Serves 6

*12 thin pancakes*
*icing sugar*
*butter for the dish*

## Filling
*6 tablespoons caster sugar*
*8 tablespoons butter*
*grated zest 1 lemon*
*3 eggs*
*1 cup curd cheese*
*¼ cup buttermilk*
*pinch salt*
*juice 1 lemon*
*1 teaspoon vanilla sugar*
*4 tablespoons seedless raisins*

## Topping
*2 eggs*
*½ cup milk*
*½ cup buttermilk*

Preheat oven to 200°C / 400°F / Gas 6 and butter a deep gratin dish. Cream butter and sugar for the filling until light and fluffy, beat in the lemon zest. Separate egg yolks and whites and beat yolks into butter mixture, one by one, then add curd cheese and buttermilk and whisk until frothy. Whisk egg whites with the pinch salt, lemon juice and vanilla sugar until stiff and fold into the mixture. Sprinkle in the raisins. Spread about two tablespoons of the mixture down the centre of each pancake and fold over. Place pancakes side by side in the prepared gratin dish. Whisk

together all the ingredients for the topping and pour over the pancakes. Bake for twelve minutes, until golden brown.

Serve warm, sprinkled with icing sugar and accompanied by a good vanilla custard or stewed morello cherries.

# Pancakes

Makes 12 pancakes

*2 eggs*
*2 teaspoons sugar*
*1 cup flour*
*2 cups milk*
*1 teaspoon vanilla extract*
*30g (1 generous oz) melted butter*
*pinch of salt*

Mix together egg and milk, and whisk in the sifted flour with a pinch of salt to make a smooth batter. Leave to stand for an hour before use. (I would now stir in a tablespoon of melted butter, but this is a question of personal preference which has not yet reached the QE2 kitchens.)

Heat a 7-inch non-stick crèpe or omelette pan over a medium heat and brush with melted butter. Pour enough of the batter into the pan to cover the pan, tipping the pan so that the batter covers the entire surface. Cook for approximately one minute, then turn the pancake over with a spatula or palette knife and cook for thirty seconds. Continue until you have used up all the batter, brushing butter over the pan before cooking each pancake and stack them as they are ready.

QE2

# Crêpes Suzette

Serves 6

*12 pancakes (see page 146)*
*2 tablespoons sugar*
*120g (4½oz) butter*
*juice of 2 oranges and 1 lemon*
*zest of 1 orange and 1 lemon*
*120ml (4½fl oz) Grand Marnier*
*60 ml (2fl oz) brandy*

Caramelize the sugar in half the butter in a flambé pan over medium heat. When the sugar has turned light brown, add remaining butter and stir until all the butter has melted. Slowly add the orange juice and then add lemon juice and grated lemon and orange zest. Fold the crêpes into four and add to the sauce. Heat the brandy and Grand Marnier in a small pan and light. Pour over the crêpes.

Serve immediately on warm plates after the flames have stopped. Top with vanilla ice-cream and whipped cream.

147

# Almond Soufflé with Raspberry Sauce

**8–10 servings**

*butter for the dish*
*2 tablespoons sugar*
*1 cup marzipan paste*
*1½ cups milk*
*3 tablespoons butter*
*3 tablespoons flour*
*pinch salt*
*¼ cup sugar*
*6 eggs*
*1 egg white*
*2 tablespoons orange liqueur*
*¼ teaspoon cream of tartar*
*Raspberry Sauce (see page 143)*

Generously butter a 2¾-litre (5-pint) soufflé dish and sprinkle with one tablespoon sugar. Knead the marzipan paste with your fingers until soft and pliable. Blend the paste with ½ cup milk in a food processor or blender until smooth and set aside. Melt butter and stir in the flour and salt, blend in remaining milk. Cook, stirring constantly, until thickened. Add the ¼ cup sugar and the marzipan mixture and heat through. Stir to blend and remove from heat.

Separate egg yolks and whites. Beat egg yolks into the marzipan mixture, one by one. Stir in orange liqueur. Leave to cool. Beat egg whites with remaining tablespoon sugar and cream of tartar until stiff. Whisk a quarter of the egg whites into the marzipan mixture and gently fold in the remainder. Pour into the prepared soufflé dish and bake at 180°C / 350°F / Gas 4 for thirty to thirty-five minutes.

To serve, pour a small amount of Raspberry Sauce on each plate and top with a portion of the soufflé.

# Vanilla Soufflé

**Makes 6 individual soufflés**

*½ litre (18fl oz ) milk*
*200g (7oz) caster sugar*
*50g (2oz) butter*
*2 vanilla pods*
*100 g (3½ oz) flour*
*10 egg yolks*
*12 egg whites*
*25g (1oz) melted butter for the ramekins*
*caster sugar for the ramekins*

Bring milk to the boil with half the sugar, the butter and vanilla pods. Tip in the flour and stir over low heat until the mixture leaves the sides of the saucepan clean. Remove from heat and allow to cool. Remove vanilla pods. Gradually mix in the egg yolks until a smooth paste has formed. This part of the recipe can be made a day in advance.

Whisk egg whites with the remaining sugar until they form soft peaks. Whisk a third of this meringue into the basic mixture, then fold in the remainder. Brush six ramekins measuring 8cm (3½ in) in diameter and 5cm (2in) high with melted butter and dust insides with caster sugar. Fill the ramekins three-quarters full. Stand the ramekins in a baking dish with water to come one-third up their sides. Bake at 200°C / 400°F / Gas 6 for twenty minutes. Serve with Chocolate Sauce or Raspberry Sauce.

# Fruit Soufflés

**Makes 6 individual soufflés**

Ingredients and method as for Vanilla Soufflé, but reduce milk by half and add 250g (9oz) fruit purée to basic mixture. Serve with Vanilla Sauce.

# Chocolate Soufflé

**Makes 6 individual soufflés**

Ingredients and method as for Vanilla Soufflé, but add 100g (3½ oz) cocoa powder and 150g (5½ oz) melted chocolate to basic mixture. Serve with Chocolate or Vanilla Sauce.

# Soufflé Rothschild

**Makes 6 individual soufflés**

Ingredients and method as for Vanilla Soufflé, but cover base of each ramekin with crumbled macaroons or diced boudoir biscuits, doused liberally with Kirsch. Top with halved stewed or tinned morello cherries or with diced glace fruit and then with the soufflé mixture.

# Raspberry Soufflé

**Serves 4 (1 large soufflé or 4 individual ones 6cm (2½ in) in diameter)**

*250ml (9fl oz) milk*
*½ vanilla pod*
*3 egg yolks*
*60g (2 generous oz) granulated sugar*
*25g (1oz) flour*
*3 tablespoons crème-de-framboise liqueur*
*icing sugar for dusting over top*
*butter and granulated sugar for coating the soufflé dishes*
*125g (4½ oz) fresh or frozen raspberries*
*30g (1 generous oz) boudoir biscuits*
*4 egg whites*
*pinch salt*

Set the milk to boil with the vanilla pod. Beat together two egg yolks with the granulated sugar, then add the sieved flour. Gradually pour the boiling milk on to the mixture, stirring it with a small whisk. Return mixture to rinsed-out saucepan, and cook for several minutes, stirring constantly. Remove from heat and stir in half the liqueur. Pour into a bowl and sprinkle top with icing sugar to prevent a skin forming. Butter soufflé dish (or dishes) and sprinkle with granulated sugar. Mash the raspberries slightly and add to soufflé cream together with remaining egg yolk.

Soak boudoir biscuits in remaining liqueur for two minutes. Whisk egg whites, with a pinch of salt, until stiff. Whisk a small quantity of the beaten egg white into the soufflé cream, then fold in remainder very gently.

Arrange half the soaked boudoir biscuits in the bottom of the soufflé dish. Spoon a little of the soufflé mixture on top and cover with remaining boudoir biscuits, then fill with remaining soufflé mixture. Smooth top with a palette knife. Start the baking process on a low setting for several minutes, then bake at 200°C / 400°C / Gas 6 for twenty to twenty-five minutes.

'Run a vegetable knife round the top to unstick the edges after some minutes,' says Chef Thierry Guimard, 'and glaze the soufflé by sprinkling with icing sugar three to four minutes before they are finished.'

# Granny Smith Apple Tart

**Serves 4**

*1 sheet puff pastry*
*10 tablespoons butter*
*10 tablespoons granulated sugar*
*1 egg*
*¼ cup cornflour*
*10 tablespoons ground almonds*
*3 medium-sized Granny Smith apples*

Cut four rounds of pastry measuring 10cm (4 in) in diameter. Place the circles on a non-stick baking sheet. Preheat oven to 190°C / 375°F / Gas 5. Cream together six tablespoons of the butter with six tablespoons of the sugar, beat in egg, cornflour and ground almonds. Refrigerate for twenty minutes. Peel, core and thinly slice the apples. Place a quarter of the almond mixture in the centre of each pastry round. Arrange apple slices on top, making a complete circle. Melt remaining butter and spoon over apples. Sprinkle with remaining sugar and bake for fifteen to twenty minutes, until golden brown and caramelized on top.

SWEET INDULGENCE

QE2

# Ginger Crème Brûlée

10 portions

*12 egg yolks*
*225g (8oz) caster sugar*
*1 litre (1¼ pints) double cream*
*15g (½ oz) fresh ginger, finely chopped*
*1 vanilla pod, split and scraped*
*good dash Grand Marnier*
*75g (3oz) caster sugar to glaze*

Whisk together egg yolks and sugar. Bring cream to boil with ginger and vanilla pod seeds. Pour cream on to lightly beaten egg yolks, add Grand Marnier and blend together. Strain mixture into ramekin dishes measuring 12cm (5in) in diameter and 3cm (1in) high. Set the dishes in a baking dish with water to come half way up the ramekins. Place in oven at 160°C / 325°F / Gas 3, until set. Remove ramekins from baking dish and leave to cool.

Sprinkle with caster sugar and glaze with a salamander or under the grill until golden brown.

# Flourless Chocolate Cake

Serves 8–10, served as a pudding with whipped cream

*450g (1lb) semi-sweet chocolate*
*(Valrhona for preference)*
*1 tablespoon vanilla extract*
*1 tablespoon dark rum*
*¾ cup strong black coffee*
*8 eggs*
*½ cup granulated sugar*
*¾ cup double cream*
*whipped cream for garnish*
*fruit berries for decoration*

Preheat oven to 150°C / 300°C /Gas 2. Butter a 25cm (10in) cake tin and refrigerate until ready to use.

Break up the chocolate into small pieces and put into a bowl, together with the vanilla extract, rum and coffee. Set the bowl over a pan of simmering water for the chocolate to melt, stirring occasionally so that there are no lumps. Turn off the heat as soon as the chocolate has melted and transfer to a larger bowl. Whisk together eggs and sugar until thick, then beat in about a quarter of the cooled chocolate mixture. Pour this mixture into the remaining chocolate mixture and blend carefully. Whip double cream until it forms soft peaks and fold into the chocolate/egg mixture with a spatula until just combined. Pour into the prepared cake tin.

Place cake tin into a roasting tin and pour in enough boiling water to come halfway up the sides of the cake tin. Bake for one hour at 150°C / 300°F / Gas 2.

Remove cake tin from the oven and let it cool at room temperature. Chill in the refrigerator overnight.

To serve, remove cake from the tin and cover top with whipped cream. Decorate with berries.

# Lemon Roulade with Citrus Fruits

Serves 6 (12 slices,
2 slices per serving)

### Roulade
*2 eggs*
*125g (4½ oz) caster sugar*
*125g (4½ oz) plain flour*

### Lemon Mousse
*2 egg yolks*
*4 lightly heaped tablespoons*
*     caster sugar*
*2 egg whites*
*1 teaspoon gelatine dissolved in a*
*     little warmed lemon juice*
*50ml (2fl oz) lemon juice*
*130ml (4½ fl oz) double cream*

### Lemon Sauce
*200ml (7fl oz) lemon juice*
*5 teaspoons caster sugar*
*2 lightly heaped tablespoons*
*     apricot jam*
*little yellow culinary colouring*

### Garnish
*Fondant icing made by creaming together 110g*
*     (4oz) butter with 110g (4oz) icing sugar*
*     and beating in 1 tablespoon lemon juice*
*halved pistachio nuts*
*candied orange and lemon segments*

To make the roulade, line a 20cm x 30cm (8in x 12in) baking sheet with buttered and floured greaseproof paper. Whisk together eggs and sugar in a bowl over simmering water until thick and fluffy. Remove from the heat, then fold in the sieved flour. Spread over prepared baking-sheet and bake at 210°C / 410°F / Gas 6 for five to seven minutes. Allow to cool and peel off greaseproof paper.

To make the mousse, whisk together egg yolk and half the sugar over steam until thickened. Remove from heat. Add gelatine dissolved in lemon juice. Whisk egg white with remaining sugar until stiff and fold into the mixture. Whisk cream into soft peaks, then fold into mixture.

To make the lemon sauce, bring the first three ingredients to the boil, mix well and leave to cool. Add a little culinary colouring.

Spread mousse over roulade and roll up. Fold into greaseproof paper and refrigerate until ready to serve. Cut roulade into twelve slices. Spread each slice with fondant icing and sprinkle with halved pistachio nuts. Garnish with candied lemon and orange segments.

SWEET INDULGENCE

QE2

# Chocolate Croissant Pudding

**Serves 6**

*150g (5½ oz) unsalted butter, melted*
*½ teaspoon powdered cinnamon*
*9 croissants*
*120g (4½ oz) chocolate chips*
*240ml (8½ fl oz) milk*
*240ml (8½ fl oz) double cream*
*4 eggs*
*2 egg yolks*
*120g (4½ oz) caster sugar*
*3 heaped tablespoons smooth apricot jam*
*        for glazing*

Mix together the melted butter and cinnamon. Cut croissants into slices and divide between six lightly buttered ovenproof dishes. Sprinkle with chocolate chips. Pour melted butter and cinnamon over croissants. Bring milk and cream to the boil. Whisk together eggs, egg yolks and sugar. Pour hot milk and cream mixture on to eggs, stir to blend and pour over croissants. Leave to stand for thirty minutes.

Stand the dishes in a roasting tin with water to come halfway up the sides and bake at 180°C/350°F/Gas 4 for thirty minutes, covering lightly with buttered aluminium foil or greaseproof paper for the last five minutes. Remove from the oven and allow to stand for a few minutes whilst preparing the apricot glaze by heating the apricot jam and passing it through a fine sieve. Brush tops of puddings with apricot glaze. Serve with ice-cream of your choice.

SWEET INDULGENCE

QE2

153

# Walnut Pudding with Whisky Sauce

Serves 6

SWEET INDULGENCE

QE2

*135g (5oz) chopped walnuts*
*25g (1oz) icing sugar*
*100g (3½ oz) butter*
*200g (7oz) caster sugar*
*3 eggs*
*200g (7oz) plain flour*
*7g (¼ oz) baking powder*
*100ml (3½ fl oz) milk*
*butter and flour for the moulds*

## Whisky Sauce

*200ml (7fl oz) single cream*
*3 egg yolks*
*1 heaped tablespoon caster sugar*
*2 tablespoons whisky*

## Garnish

*500ml (1lb 2oz) sugar*
*100ml (3½ fl oz) water*
*18 walnut halves*
*140g (5oz) strawberries*
*70g (2½ oz) blueberries*

Spread the chopped walnuts on a baking sheet and sprinkle with the icing sugar. Place in oven at 180°C / 350°F / Gas 4 until the sugar has melted and turned golden brown. Remove from oven and set to cool.

Cream butter and sugar until light and fluffy, beat in the eggs. Sieve together flour and baking powder and add to mixture. Finally add the milk. Butter and lightly flour six dariole moulds each holding 125ml (4½ fl oz). Spoon mixture into prepared moulds and set them in a roasting tin with water to come a quarter way up the sides. Bake at 180°C / 350°F / Gas 4, for twenty to twenty-five minutes. Once a skin has formed – after about ten minutes – place tin foil over the puddings to keep the steam in and complete the baking.

To make the whisky sauce, bring cream to boil. Beat together egg yolks and sugar. Pour boiling cream on to egg yolks and return to rinsed-out saucepan. Cook gently – not allowing the sauce to boil and stirring all the time – until sauce covers back of a cooking spoon. Remove from heat and stir in the whisky.

To make the garnish, boil the sugar with the water until it turns to caramel – let the sugar dissolve in the water first before turning up the heat. Plunge the saucepan into a bowl of ice-cold water for a few seconds to stop the sugar from getting any darker. Spear each walnut half with a cocktail stick and dip into the caramel. Pull out quickly so that a thin thread forms, running from the walnut.

Invert puddings on to plates and arrange fruit and walnut halves around it. Top with whisky sauce.

# Chocolate Mousse Cake

Makes two cakes (46cm/18in diameter)

## Sugar Syrup
*170g (6 oz) caster sugar*
*80ml (3fl oz) water*
*2 tablespoons of Kirsch*

## Cakes
*2 teaspoons powdered instant coffee*
*1 teaspoon hot water*
*4 eggs*
*125g (4½ oz) caster sugar*
*12 flat tablespoons flour*
*2 lightly heaped tablespoons cocoa powder*
*2 tablespoons melted butter*
*cocoa powder for sprinkling*
*white chocolate for decoration*

## For the Mousse
*240g (8½ oz) dark couverture chocolate*
*7 egg yolks*
*5 lightly heaped tablespoons*
     *caster sugar*
*2 teaspoons powdered gelatine*
*1 teaspoon instant coffee*
*700ml (1¼ pints) double cream*
*100ml (3½ fl oz) Kahlua liqueur*

To make the sugar syrup, dissolve the sugar in water and bring to the boil. Simmer for ten minutes then remove from heat. Allow to cool then add the Kirsch.

To make the cakes, dissolve instant coffee in hot water. Leave to cool. Whisk together eggs and sugar over a pan of simmering water until thick and fluffy. Add dissolved instant coffee. Remove from heat and whisk until cold. Sift together flour and cocoa and fold into egg mixture. Finally fold in the melted but not hot butter.

Bake in a buttered and floured 46cm (18in) cake tin at 180°C / 350°F / Gas 4 for thirty-five minutes. Remove from cake tin and set to cool on a rack.

To make the mousse, break the chocolate into small pieces and set to melt either over a pan of simmering water or in a low oven. Whisk together egg yolks and sugar over a pan of simmering water until thick and fluffy. Remove from heat and whisk until cold. Add melted but not hot chocolate. Dissolve moistened gelatine and instant coffee in hot Kahlua liqueur and add. Whisk cream until it holds soft peaks and fold into the mixture.

Cut through the cake once and place halves on plates. Put a flan ring around each cake. Sprinkle cakes with sugar syrup. Spread mousse evenly over each cake and refrigerate for two hours. Dust with cocoa powder and decorate with white chocolate discs or shavings.

SWEET INDULGENCE

QE2

# P.S.

## By Gretel Beer

I met James Villas, 'one of the most knowledgeable, readable and trustworthy writers on the subject of food in America today' (Craig Claiborne) on a transatlantic crossing. It was my fifth. And his sixty-third. Or perhaps his sixty-fourth – he'd lost count somewhere 'en routes'. 'Going on board the QE2 is still the most glamorous dining experience anywhere. When I walk into the Queen's Grill I get a shimmer of fairyland where the word "NO" does not exist,' he enthused. 'Everything is correct. Perfect. Sometimes I order a simple dish like an omelette, just to relish this perfection. I've never had omelettes – not even in France – to equal those turned out by the dozen in the Princess Grill'. (He had previously named the Princess Grill the finest restaurant in the world and only transferred his allegiance to the Queen's Grill when David Chambers transferred as Maître d'.)

'And it is the only place in the world where you can consume unlimited amounts of fresh Iranian caviar – morning, noon and night – for no more than the price of a first-class ticket. And for those who don't know, even inordinate amounts of caviar have relatively few calories. In fact, on one occasion I crossed the Atlantic on the QE2 for the sole purpose of losing weight painlessly. I knocked off six ugly pounds in five days by 'surviving' on a diet of melon, cold lobster, truffled pheasant, asparagus and heaven knows how many three-ounce crocks of fresh caviar. And that was when the crossing stretched over five days – I might have lost another pound or two on the present six-day crossing.'

James Villas summed it up in a nutshell – the glamour, luxury and sheer perfection of the food on the QE2 – and if I had not been half-way through the work on this book, this would have inspired me to start it there and then. In fact I had started planning it years ago – when Rudi Sodamin became Executive (and later Corporate Executive) Chef and changed the menus completely – from being dependable, predictable and – let's face it – a little dull ('banqueting on the ocean wave') to glamorous, exciting and worthy of a Michelin-starred restaurant on land. His successors – Corporate Executive Chef Karl Muehlberger and Executive Chef Karl Winkler (who returned to the QE2 after work on other Cunard ships) carried on and embellished these brilliant menus – supported by five Chefs and over a hundred cooks. And I cannot thank them enough for their tremendous help with this book. (An extra 'thank you' to Seamus – we never learned his surname – who was forever present, smoothing our path when it came to tricky locations – or tricky adaptations of recipes ).

Very special thanks to John Duffy – Hotel Manager since 1981 and only the third since the QE2 was launched – for giving us a free run of the ship and arranging the photography without the slightest disruption to passengers who treated our exploits as part of the entertainment programme – and for having the grace to greet us with 'welcome home' on each trip! And to his secretaries Jacqui Nicol and Beverley Maclean – the latter for teaching me how to use a word processor in mid-ocean without fusing the electricity of the entire ship. To Eric Flounders and Michael Gallagher at Cunard's London office for coping with our – usually impossible – requests at short notice and not raising an eyebrow (at least not a visible one) when I urgently asked for a giant Haggis to be shipped on board on the day of departure. And to Peter Tobler, Director of Food and Beverage Operations for allowing it all to happen.

My very special thanks to British Airways for flying us and our ever increasing luggage (sixteen pieces of photographic equipment at the last count) and for introducing me to the supreme comfort of their Sleeper Service – the most luxurious cosseting I've ever experienced and as good as a holiday – the perfect ending to a transatlantic crossing on the QE2.

And last, but not least to Lesley and Laurie Evans for doing all the hard work (Lesley did all the styling for photography) to produce these splendid pictures – whilst I had all the pleasure of tasting and selecting the dishes.

# Some Culinary Definitions

| British | American |
|---|---|
| aubergine | eggplant |
| bicarbonate of soda | baking soda |
| clingfilm | plastic film |
| coriander | cilantro |
| cornflour | cornstarch |
| double cream | heavy cream |
| essence | extract |
| fillet | tenderloin |
| frying pan | skillet |
| gelatine | gelatin |
| greaseproof paper | waxed paper |
| grill | broil |
| haricot beans | Boston/navy beans |
| icing | frosting |
| icing sugar | confectioner's sugar |
| minced (meat) | ground (meat) |
| plain flour | all purpose flour |
| polenta | cornmeal |
| prawns | shrimps |
| pumpkin | summer squash |
| spring onion | scallion |
| single cream | light cream |
| sweetcorn | corn |
| tinned | canned |
| tomato purée | tomato paste |
| vanilla pod | vanilla bean |

# Weights, Measures and Material

All butter used is unsalted butter unless otherwise stated.

All flour used is plain flour unless otherwise stated.

1 cup equals 225ml (8 fl oz)

All pints are imperial pints which equal 20 fl oz.

Do not mix metric and imperial measures in the same recipe – use either throughout.

# Index

Page numbers in **bold type** are where you'll find recipes, and in *italic type* where you'll find sumptuous full-page photographs. Other entries refer to ingredients and tips.

INDEX

QE2